9 SELF-CARE ESSENTIALS

Mastering Mindfulness, Emotional Wellness, and Self-Love for a Balanced, Stress-Free, and Empowered Life

Eliza Bennet

For more information or to book an event, contact :

help@inspireself-growth.com

http://www.inspireself-growth.com

Book design by PageMaster Pro

Cover design by CoverStory Artistry

ISBN - Paperback: 9798877002197

ISBN - Hardcover: 9798877593732

First Edition February 2024

Contents

Preface

Welcome to a journey that intertwines the personal with the universal – an exploration of self-care, emotional wellness, and personal growth. This book is a guide and a companion on your path to understanding and nurturing your mind, body, and soul.

Within these pages, we delve into mindfulness, emotional wellness, stress management, and the transformative journey of self-love and inner peace. Each chapter blends insightful knowledge with practical applications to enrich your daily life.

While based on real experiences, the narratives shared here have had names and details altered to respect individual privacy. These stories are windows into the lives of those who have navigated the path of self-discovery and transformation, offering both inspiration and resonance with your own journey.

This book is for anyone seeking a pause from life's bustle, those yearning for a deeper self-connection, and those aspiring to a life of fulfillment and joy. It's an invitation to embark on a journey of self-discovery, resilience, and renewed purpose.

As you engage with this book, I encourage you to reflect, practice, and be inspired. Remember, personal growth is a continuous journey unique to each individual. Let this book be a step towards a more mindful, peaceful, and fulfilling life.

So, let us begin this journey together, embracing discovery, transformation, and a deeper understanding of ourselves and the world around us.

Introduction: The Journey of Self-Care

"The most powerful relationship you will ever have is the relationship with yourself. You wake up with yourself, and you go to bed with yourself. How you treat yourself, how you talk to yourself, and how you nurture yourself deeply impacts every area of your life. Your relationship with yourself sets the tone for every other relationship you have. Invest in understanding yourself, caring for yourself, and respecting yourself. This is the essence of self-care, and it's the most substantial investment you can make." – (Maraboli, 2014)

Steve Maraboli is a renowned life coach, motivational speaker, and bestselling author known for his insights into human behavior and personal development.

Introduction: The Journey of Self-Care

Imagine awakening each morning not just to the sound of your alarm but to a feeling of deep rejuvenation and balance. Picture yourself greeting each day not with a sense of dread for the challenges ahead but with a heart full of optimism and a mind equipped with resilience. This isn't a scenario reserved for the few; it's a tangible, achievable state of being that awaits you.

Welcome to a transformative journey where what was once extraordinary becomes your new normal. In this world, stress is not a relentless enemy but a manageable aspect of life, transformed into moments of serenity. Here, self-care is not just a buzzword but your newfound superpower, unlocking a life of harmony and fulfillment.

This book isn't just a collection of self-help pages; it's a gateway to a life of enriched well-being, a life where self-care transcends being a luxury and becomes as essential and natural as breathing. Take a deep, life-affirming breath and step into a realm where nurturing yourself lays the foundation for a vibrant, fulfilling existence.

Redefining Self-Care: A Comprehensive Approach

Steve Maraboli once beautifully said that self-care is about nurturing the most important relationship you have – the one with yourself. This book aims to shatter the myths that shroud self-care, often misconstrued as mere indulgences like extravagant spa days or retail therapy. True self-care is an all-encompassing practice that attends to the mind, body, and spirit, involving conscious choices and actions that foster your physical vitality, emotional stability, and mental clarity.

Our exploration delves deep, uncovering the profound layers of true self-care. We perceive it as a multifaceted gem, each facet representing an essential element of your well-being. From the grounding practices of mindfulness to the rejuvenating power of physical activities, from emotional nourishment to the exploration of your spiritual depths, this book is a holistic guide to understanding, caring for, and respecting your whole self – the cornerstone upon which all other relationships are built.

The Urgent Need for Self-Care in Today's World

In our fast-paced, digitally driven era, where work and personal life often intertwine indistinguishably, stress, anxiety, and burnout have become prevalent currencies. The recent global upheavals, especially the COVID-19 pandemic, have cast a glaring spotlight on the importance of self-care. These challenges have not only disrupted lives but also amplified stress and underscored the fragile nature of mental health. In such times, adopting a self-care routine is not just beneficial; it's essential for maintaining balance, resilience, and a semblance of normalcy.

Moreover, as the world awakens to the importance of health and wellness, the role of mental health is gaining unprecedented recognition. Self-care has shifted from a perceived indulgence to an acknowledged necessity in navigating the complexities of modern life. It equips us to face life's hurdles with agility and grace, building a resilience that is more vital today than ever before.

Guiding You on Your Self-Care Journey

Consider this book your personal guide and companion on your self-care journey. Each chapter, rich in both theory and practice, focuses on a different dimension of self-care. These chapters are carefully crafted, not just to inform but to bring about transformation – to turn knowledge into a living, breathing part of your daily existence. They are meticulously structured, guiding you in creating a self-care routine that resonates with your unique needs and life circumstances.

As you immerse yourself in these pages, you'll discover the secrets hidden in plain sight – practical, straightforward strategies that can effortlessly intertwine with the tapestry of your daily life. You'll learn the art of tuning into your body and mind, embracing self-dialogue filled with kindness, and facing life's tumultuous moments with an inner calmness born from within.

Are you ready to turn the page? Ready to embark on a path of learning, growth, and profound transformation? Your journey to self-care, to a life brimming with joy and balance, starts now. Let us take this first step together into the world of mindfulness, where each breath is an opportunity for renewal and each moment a chance to thrive anew.

1: Mindfulness – The Foundation of Self-Care

"The present moment is filled with joy and happiness. If you are attentive, you will see it. In our busy lives, we often overlook the simple beauty that surrounds us in the here and now. When we pause, breathe, and truly inhabit the present, we open ourselves to the vast richness of experience. This awareness is the first step to transforming our everyday experiences into moments of joy and fulfillment." – (Hạnh, 2013)

Thich Nhat Hanh was, and still is a revered Vietnamese Zen Buddhist monk, peace activist, and mindfulness advocate. His teachings have influenced millions worldwide, emphasizing the importance of mindfulness and compassion in everyday life.

Chapter 1: Mindfulness – The Foundation of Self-Care

Pause for a moment. Yes, right now. Notice the rhythm of your breath, the gentle rise and fall of your chest, the subtle sounds surrounding you, the sensation of being alive in this very instant. This is where our journey into mindfulness begins. In a world that's constantly rushing forward, mindfulness invites us to do something revolutionary: to stop, to breathe, to be fully present. It's not about silencing your thoughts or escaping reality; it's about awakening to the richness of the here and now.

In this chapter, we'll explore how the simple, yet profound practice of mindfulness can transform your everyday experiences, enhance your connection with yourself and others, and create a space of clarity and calm in the hustle of daily life. Are you ready to explore how mindfulness can change moments of your day and the essence of how you experience life? Let's embark on this journey together, one mindful breath at a time.

Understanding Mindfulness

While deeply rooted in ancient traditions, the profound practice of mindfulness remains remarkably relevant and beneficial in our fast-paced, modern world. The late renowned mindfulness teacher Thich Nhat Hanh, who left an indelible mark on the world with his teachings, emphasized the transformative power of being fully present and engaged in the moment without judgment. This chapter explores the depths of mindfulness, unpacking its origins, benefits, and practical applications in everyday life.

The Roots and Evolution of Mindfulness

Mindfulness finds its roots in Buddhist meditation, which dates back thousands of years. Originally, mindfulness was a means of fostering spiritual awareness and enlightenment. In Buddhism, it is part of the Eightfold Path, a guide to ethical and mindful living. However, the essence of mindfulness transcends religious boundaries, making it universally applicable and beneficial.

In the 20th century, mindfulness was adapted into a secular practice, thanks partly to pioneers like Jon Kabat-Zinn, who founded the Mindfulness-Based Stress Reduction (MBSR) program. This adaptation has made mindfulness accessible to a broader audience, irrespective of their spiritual beliefs or backgrounds.

Mindfulness Defined

Mindfulness is the practice of paying full attention to the present moment with an attitude of openness, curiosity, and non-judgment. It involves being aware of your thoughts, feelings, bodily sensations, and the surrounding environment. This awareness allows you to observe your experiences without getting caught up in them. It's about noticing the mind's tendency to wander and gently guiding it back to the present.

Scientific Backing and Benefits

Modern science has taken a keen interest in mindfulness, with numerous studies underscoring its benefits. Research indicates that regular mindfulness practice can lead to:

- **Reduced Stress:** Mindfulness helps in downregulating the body's stress response, leading to decreased levels of cortisol, the stress hormone.
- **Enhanced Mental Clarity and Attention:** By training the brain to focus on the present, mindfulness can improve concentration and cognitive flexibility.
- **Lowered Anxiety Levels:** Mindfulness creates a space between stimuli and our reactions, allowing for better emotional regulation and reduced anxiety.

- **Improved Physical Health:** Studies suggest that mindfulness can positively impact heart health, reduce chronic pain, and boost the immune system.
- **Greater Overall Well-Being:** Mindfulness is linked to increased happiness, greater empathy, and improved relationships.

Practical Mindfulness Techniques for Daily Life

Incorporating mindfulness into your daily life doesn't necessarily mean setting aside hours for meditation. Mindfulness can be seamlessly integrated into your routine through simple, effective techniques. These practices help anchor you in the present moment, enhancing your day-to-day experience and overall well-being.

1. Mindful Breathing

Mindful breathing is a fundamental technique that can be practised anywhere, at any time. It involves focusing your attention on your breath, the natural ebb and flow of inhaling and exhaling.

How to Practice:

- Find a comfortable position. You can do this sitting, standing, or even lying down.
- Close your eyes if it helps you focus.
- Take a deep breath in, and slowly exhale. Pay attention to the sensation of air entering and leaving your nostrils or moving in and out of your lungs.
- Notice the rise and fall of your chest or the expansion and contraction of your abdomen with each breath.
- When your mind wanders, gently bring your focus back to your breath.

- Start with just a minute or two and gradually increase the duration.

Benefits: This practice can calm the mind, reduce stress, and bring a sense of inner peace. It's particularly effective in moments of high stress or anxiety, offering an immediate anchor to the present moment.

2. Mindful Eating

Mindful eating turns a daily necessity into an opportunity for mindfulness practice. It involves fully experiencing the act of eating, paying attention to the sensory experiences of your meal.

How to Practice:

- Begin by looking at your food, noticing the colors and textures.
- As you eat, pay attention to the flavors, textures, and aromas of each bite.
- Chew slowly, savoring each mouthful.
- Notice the sensation of hunger subsiding and fullness arising.
- Acknowledge your body's cues of hunger and satiety to guide when you start and stop eating.

Benefits: Mindful eating can enhance your enjoyment of food, prevent overeating, and improve digestion. It encourages a healthier, more conscious relationship with food.

3. Mindful Walking

Mindful walking is about walking with awareness. It turns an ordinary activity into a practice of mindfulness, allowing you to connect with the present moment in a dynamic way.

How to Practice:

- Begin by standing still, noticing the weight of your body pressing down onto your feet.
- As you start to walk, focus on the sensation of your feet touching and leaving the ground.
- Observe the rhythm of your steps. Is your pace fast, slow, or moderate?
- Become aware of your surroundings – the sights, sounds, and smells.
- If your mind starts to wander, gently bring your attention back to the physical sensation of walking.

Benefits: Mindful walking can be a great way to break up long periods of sitting, reduce feelings of stress or restlessness, and connect more deeply with your environment.

4. Mindful Listening

Mindful listening is about fully engaging with the act of listening, whether to another person, music, or the sounds of your environment. It involves being fully present and attentive, without judgment or distraction.

How to Practice:

- In conversation, focus entirely on the speaker. Notice their words, tone, and body language.
- Resist the urge to formulate your response while listening; instead, truly hear what's being said.
- When listening to music or environmental sounds, close your eyes and let yourself fully absorb and experience the sounds.
- Acknowledge any thoughts or judgments that arise, then gently redirect your attention back to listening.

Benefits: Mindful listening can improve communication, strengthen relationships, and increase your appreciation and enjoyment of music and nature.

5. Mindful Observation

This practice involves choosing an object and focusing your entire attention on it. It can be anything in your environment – a plant, a cup of coffee, a piece of artwork.

How to Practice:

- Select an object and look at it as if you're seeing it for the first time.
- Observe its shape, color, texture, and any other qualities.
- Notice the light and shadows, the nuances of its appearance.
- If your mind wanders, gently bring it back to observing the object.

Benefits: This practice enhances your ability to concentrate and appreciate the beauty in ordinary things, fostering a deeper connection with your surroundings.

6. Mindful Gratitude

Practicing gratitude mindfully involves consciously acknowledging things you're grateful for in life. This can range from significant relationships to simple pleasures.

How to Practice:

- Take a few moments each day to think of things you're grateful for.
- Reflect on why you're thankful for these things and how they impact your life.
- You can also keep a gratitude journal, writing down a few things each day.

Benefits: This practice fosters positive emotions, reduces stress, and can shift your perspective to a more optimistic outlook on life.

Incorporating Mindfulness into Daily Activities

Integrating mindfulness into various activities throughout your day can significantly enhance your experience of life, bringing a sense of calm, focus, and fulfillment to routine tasks. Let's explore how you can infuse mindfulness into everyday activities like exercising, cooking, and working.

1. Mindfulness in Exercise

Exercise is not just a physical activity; it's an opportunity to cultivate mindfulness. Whether you're jogging, practicing yoga, or lifting weights, being mindful during exercise can deepen your connection with your body and improve your overall workout experience.

How to Practice:

- Focus on your body movements and the sensations in each muscle group. Feel the stretch, the strength, and the exertion.
- Pay attention to your breathing – how it deepens with intense exercise and calms during cool-downs.
- Notice your thoughts during the workout. Are they encouraging or self-critical? Practice observing these thoughts without attachment.

Benefits: Mindful exercise can increase body awareness, reduce the risk of injury, and enhance the enjoyment of physical activity. It also helps in managing exercise-related mental blocks.

2. Mindfulness in Cooking

Cooking can be a delightful mindfulness exercise. It's an activity that engages all your senses, making it perfect for practicing present-moment awareness.

How to Practice:

- As you prepare ingredients, notice their color, texture, and aroma.

- Be fully present as you chop, stir, or sauté. Observe the sounds of cooking and the transformation of ingredients.

- Treat cooking as a peaceful, meditative practice rather than a rushed chore.

Benefits: Mindful cooking can turn meal preparation into a relaxing and creative activity, helping you to appreciate the food and the process of making it.

3. Mindfulness at Work

The workplace can be a hectic environment, but it also offers numerous opportunities for mindfulness practice.

How to Practice:

- Begin your workday with a few minutes of mindful breathing to set a calm, focused tone.

- During tasks, try to single-task rather than multi-task. Fully immerse yourself in one task at a time.

- Take short, mindful breaks to reset. A few moments of focusing on your breath or observing your surroundings can be refreshing.

Benefits: Mindfulness at work can improve concentration, reduce stress, and foster better relationships with colleagues. It can also enhance decision-making and creativity.

The Ripple Effect of Mindful Living

Consistently practicing mindfulness in daily activities cultivates a habit of living in the present. This approach can gradually transform your experience of life, leading to deeper peace, heightened awareness, and greater fulfillment. It's about finding joy and contentment in the ordinary moments, understanding that each moment is an opportunity to be fully alive.

As you practice mindfulness in various aspects of your life, you may start noticing subtle but significant changes. You might find yourself responding to stress more calmly, enjoying simple pleasures more deeply, and feeling more connected to yourself and others.

Mindfulness is not a destination; it's a way of being. The more you practice, the more natural it becomes, and the richer your experience of life grows.

Remember, mindfulness is a journey, not a race. Be patient with yourself and embrace each moment with openness and curiosity.

Overcoming Common Challenges in Practicing Mindfulness

While mindfulness offers numerous benefits, many individuals encounter challenges when trying to incorporate it into their daily lives. Understanding and overcoming these challenges is crucial for developing a consistent and rewarding mindfulness practice.

1. Dealing with a Wandering Mind

A common hurdle in mindfulness is dealing with a mind that constantly wanders. This is a natural aspect of the human mind and not a failure in practicing mindfulness.

Strategies for Overcoming the Wandering Mind:

- Acknowledge when your mind has wandered without judgment. Gently guide it back to the present moment.
- Use anchoring techniques to maintain presence, such as focusing on your breath or bodily sensations.

- Practice regularly. Like any skill, mindfulness improves with practice. Over time, you'll find it easier to maintain focus.

Insight: Remember that the act of noticing your mind has wandered and bringing it back to the present is the practice of mindfulness.

2. Finding Time for Mindfulness

Many people struggle to find time for mindfulness in their busy schedules. However, mindfulness doesn't always require dedicated time; it can be integrated into daily activities.

Strategies for Overcoming:

- Start with short practices. Even a minute of mindful breathing can be beneficial.
- Incorporate mindfulness into routine activities like showering, eating, or commuting.
- Set reminders to take brief mindfulness breaks throughout your day.

Insight: Mindfulness is less about carving out new time and more about being present in your existing activities.

3. Unrealistic Expectations

Some practitioners expect immediate results from mindfulness, such as instant stress relief or a profound sense of peace. Having realistic expectations and understanding that benefits accrue over time is important.

Strategies for Overcoming:

- Be patient with yourself and the process. Mindfulness is a journey, not a quick fix.

- Celebrate small victories, like noticing a slight improvement in your stress levels or increased moments of joy.
- Understand that mindfulness is a varied experience; some days will be easier than others.

Insight: The real power of mindfulness lies in steady, gradual progress.

4. Physical Discomfort During Practice

Sitting still for mindfulness practices like meditation can sometimes be uncomfortable or challenging, especially for beginners.

Strategies for Overcoming:

- Choose a comfortable posture. Mindfulness can be practiced sitting, standing, lying down or even walking.
- Make small adjustments as needed for your comfort. Mindfulness is about awareness, not endurance.
- Start with short sessions and gradually increase the duration as your comfort level improves.

Insight: The aim is to be mindful, not to achieve a perfect posture.

5. Self-Judgment

Often, practitioners judge themselves harshly for "not doing mindfulness correctly" or for having "too many thoughts."

Strategies for Overcoming:

- Understand that mindfulness is a non-judgmental practice. The goal is to observe your thoughts and feelings without criticism.
- Treat yourself with kindness and compassion. Self-criticism is counterproductive to mindfulness.

- Recognize that every practitioner experiences challenges. You are not alone in your struggles.

Insight: Mindfulness is as much about the attitude with which you approach the practice as it is about the practice itself.

By addressing these challenges head-on and adjusting your approach to mindfulness, you can develop a more enjoyable and effective practice. Remember, mindfulness is a personal and individual experience. What matters most is finding a practice that works for you and contributes to your overall well-being.

Mindful Moments: Sarah's Journey to a Calmer Life

Meet 'Sarah', a story of transformation that beautifully illustrates the power of integrating mindfulness into a bustling lifestyle. Sarah, a marketing executive in her mid-thirties, lived her life at a breakneck pace. Her daily routine was a whirlwind of early morning alarms, back-to-back meetings, and late-night work sessions. Her life was a constant race against the clock, with weekends blurring into weekdays in a never-ending cycle of commitments and deadlines.

Sarah's journey towards mindfulness began almost inadvertently. During a routine health check-up, her elevated stress levels couldn't be ignored. It was clear that the constant pressure was taking its toll, both physically and emotionally. Her doctor's suggestion of mindfulness initially seemed impractical to Sarah. The thought of carving out time for meditation seemed like another task in her already overflowing schedule.

However, the seed was planted, and Sarah's curiosity about mindfulness grew. She started experimenting with incorporating small mindfulness practices into her daily routine. The first change was during her morning commute. Instead of filling her car with the sounds of early morning conference calls, she turned off her phone and focused on mindful breathing at traffic stops. Each red light became a reminder to pause and breathe. She would close her eyes, take deep breaths, and pay attention to the rhythm, noticing its calming effect on her mind and body.

Lunchtime presented another opportunity. Sarah swapped her desk lunches for short walks. She would step outside, leaving her phone behind, and walk mindfully. Each step was a chance to connect with the present moment. She focused on the feel of the pavement under her feet, the rustling of leaves, and the distant hum of city life. These walks became an oasis of tranquility during her chaotic day.

The changes were gradual but profound. Sarah began to notice a shift in her stress levels. The morning commute was no longer a source of tension but a time for calm. Her walks infused her afternoons with a renewed sense of energy and focus. She found herself more present and engaged, both in her personal and professional life.

Her colleagues started noticing too. Sarah's interactions became more thoughtful, and her responses more considered. She brought a sense of calm to her team, which had a ripple effect on their productivity and overall morale.

But the most significant change was in Sarah's own perception of her life. She no longer felt like she was constantly racing against time. Mindfulness taught her to find moments of peace amidst the chaos, to appreciate the present without constantly worrying about the next item on her to-do list. She learned that self-care wasn't a luxury but a necessity for her well-being and happiness.

Sarah's story is a testament to the fact that mindfulness doesn't require drastic changes or additional time. It's about weaving moments of awareness into the fabric of our daily lives. It's a gentle reminder that in the midst of our busy lives, there's always an opportunity to pause, breathe, and connect with the present moment.

As we close this chapter on mindfulness, you've begun to see how powerful being present in the moment can be. You've learned to breathe through the chaos, to find peace in the now, and to embrace life one mindful step at a time. But our journey doesn't end here. With the foundation of mindfulness firmly laid, we're ready to delve deeper into the landscapes of our inner world.

In the next chapter, we turn our attention to Emotional Wellness – a realm where mindfulness will serve as a guiding light. Here, we'll explore how to navigate the complex tapestry of our emotions. From the peaks of joy to the valleys of sorrow, understanding and managing our emotional world is crucial for a balanced, fulfilling life. We'll learn to recognize our feelings, embrace them without judgment, and use them as a compass to guide our decisions and actions.

2: Emotional Wellness – Navigating Your Inner World

"The curious paradox is that when I accept myself just as I am, then I can change. It is only when I begin to truly understand and embrace my own feelings, my own experiences, and my own existence, without judgement or denial, that transformation becomes possible. This acceptance does not mean complacency; rather, it is the first step in allowing growth and healing to occur."– (Rogers, 1961)

Carl R. Rogers, a distinguished American psychologist and one of the founders of the humanistic approach to psychology, profoundly influenced our understanding of the self and personal growth.

Chapter 2: Emotional Wellness – Navigating Your Inner World

Welcome to the world within you, a universe as vast and complex as any star-filled sky. Here, in the realm of Emotional Wellness, we embark on an odyssey to discover and understand the full spectrum of our emotions. This chapter is more than just a journey; it explores the essence of what makes us human. Imagine having the map to navigate through the intricate labyrinth of your emotions, turning every twist and turn into an opportunity for growth and self-discovery. From the gentle whispers of joy to the thunderous echoes of anger, every emotion you experience is a piece of the puzzle that is uniquely you.

In this chapter, we don't just learn to face our emotions; we learn to dance with them, to embrace their ebb and flow with grace and resilience. So, are you ready to dive deep into the waters of your emotional world to uncover the pearls of wisdom that lie within? Let's begin this transformative journey together, learning to navigate our emotions not as challenges to be overcome but as allies on the path to a more fulfilling and balanced life.

The Pillars of Emotional Wellness

Emotional wellness is a multifaceted concept deeply rooted in how we perceive, experience, and manage our emotions. Building upon Carl R. Rogers' insightful perspective on self-acceptance, let's delve deeper into the pillars of emotional wellness.

1. Self-Awareness

Self-awareness is the foundational element of emotional wellness. It entails a deep understanding of your emotional reactions, the triggers that provoke them, and the habitual patterns they form. This process of introspection is vital for recognizing how your emotions play a significant role in shaping your thoughts, decisions, and behaviors.

Understanding your emotional responses is critical to managing them effectively. For instance, recognizing that certain environments make you anxious allows you to prepare or avoid such settings. Similarly, knowing that particular topics make you joyful can lead you to seek out conversations or activities that involve them.

Practical Application: Cultivating Self-Awareness

Developing self-awareness is a vital step in understanding and managing your emotions. Here are some detailed methods to enhance self-awareness:

a. **Regular Check-ins:**

The practice of regular check-ins involves pausing at various times throughout the day to introspectively assess your emotional state.

How to Implement:

- Set specific times or use certain activities as reminders to check in with yourself. This could be during your morning routine, before meals, or when transitioning between different tasks.
- Ask yourself questions like, "How am I feeling right now?" or "What's my mood at this moment?" Try to name your emotions as precisely as possible.
- Acknowledge the feelings without judgment. Whether you're feeling happy, stressed, anxious, or excited, recognize that these emotions are part of your experience.

b. Emotional Journaling:

Emotional journaling is a powerful tool for tracking your feelings and the situations that trigger them. It can provide insight into your emotional patterns and reactions.

How to Implement:

- Dedicate a notebook or digital document for your emotional journal. Choose a format that feels most comfortable and accessible for you.
- Write about your day and specifically focus on moments that evoked strong emotional responses. Describe the situation, your feelings, and any physical sensations associated with those emotions.
- Over time, review your entries to identify any patterns or triggers. This can reveal insights into how certain environments, interactions, or thoughts influence your emotional state.

c. Mindfulness Meditation:

Mindfulness meditation is a practice that involves focusing your attention on the present moment and observing your thoughts and feelings without judgment. It can enhance your ability to recognize and understand your emotions.

How to Implement:

- Find a quiet and comfortable space where you can sit without interruption. Allocate a regular time each day for this practice.
- Start with just a few minutes of meditation and gradually increase the duration as you become more comfortable with the practice.
- As you meditate, observe any emotions that arise. Acknowledge these feelings and let them pass without getting attached to them.

This practice can help in understanding your emotional responses in a deeper way.

- Focus on your breath or a mantra as a way to anchor your attention. When your mind wanders, gently bring it back to your chosen point of focus.

By incorporating these practices into your daily routine, you can significantly enhance your self-awareness. This increased awareness is a crucial step towards managing your emotions effectively and improving your overall emotional wellness.

2. Self-Acceptance

Carl Rogers' concept of self-acceptance is a crucial component of emotional wellness. It's the practice of embracing all facets of your being — your strengths and achievements, as well as your flaws and shortcomings. Self-acceptance is about understanding that imperfection is part of the human condition and that acknowledging and accepting these aspects of yourself is vital to emotional health and personal growth.

Self-acceptance is not about resigning to your faults but rather about acknowledging them without self-judgment. This acknowledgment creates a space for growth and change. When you accept yourself, you create an environment of self-love where personal development can flourish.

Practical Application: Developing Self-Acceptance

Cultivating self-acceptance is a critical aspect of emotional wellness. It involves embracing every part of yourself, including your flaws and mistakes. Here are some detailed methods to enhance self-acceptance:

a. Affirmations:

Affirmations are positive statements that can help you challenge and overcome negative thoughts. When repeated often, they can start to make a positive change in your self-esteem and overall outlook.

How to Implement:

- Write down a list of positive affirmations that resonate with your personal challenges and goals for self-acceptance. Examples include "I am worthy just as I am" or "I embrace all parts of myself."
- Recite these affirmations daily, preferably first thing in the morning or before going to bed. Saying them out loud in front of a mirror can be particularly effective.
- Whenever you encounter a negative thought about yourself, counteract it by repeating an affirmation.

b. Self-Compassion:

Self-compassion involves treating yourself with the same kindness, concern, and support you'd offer a good friend.

How to Implement:

- Practice mindfulness to recognize and accept your thoughts and feelings without judgment.
- When you notice self-critical thoughts, pause and reframe them as if you were talking to a friend. Ask yourself, "Would I say this to someone I care about?" If not, how would you rephrase it?
- Engage in self-care activities that promote well-being, like reading a book, taking a bath, or engaging in a hobby.

c. Reflective Exercises:

Reflective exercises can help you focus on your positive qualities and achievements, fostering a greater sense of self-acceptance.

How to Implement:

- Set aside time each week to reflect on your positive traits and accomplishments. Write these down in a journal.
- Consider writing a letter to yourself, highlighting your strengths, achievements, and the challenges you've overcome.
- Reflect on your growth and progress over time, acknowledging how you've developed and learned from past experiences.

d. Forgiveness:

Forgiving yourself is a necessary part of self-acceptance. It involves letting go of past regrets and understanding that mistakes are part of the human experience.

How to Implement:

- Acknowledge and accept your mistakes instead of suppressing or denying them.
- Understand that everyone makes mistakes, which are opportunities for learning and growth.
- Consider writing a forgiveness letter to yourself. Detail what you are forgiving yourself for and why, and express understanding and compassion.

By actively working on these practices, you cultivate a stronger sense of self-acceptance. This not only improves your relationship with yourself but also enhances your interactions with others, contributing to a more emotionally healthy and fulfilling life.

3. Resilience

Resilience is often described as the mental reservoir of strength that people are able to call on in times of need to carry them through without falling apart. It's fundamentally about adapting well in the face of adversity, trauma, tragedy, threats, or significant sources of stress. This adaptability is fundamental for emotional wellness, as it enables you to face challenges head-on, learn from them, and emerge stronger.

Practical Application: Developing Resilience

Resilience is your emotional toughness, the ability to recover quickly from difficulties and adapt well to change. It's not about avoiding challenges but learning how to deal with them effectively. Here are practical ways to build and strengthen your resilience:

a. Set Realistic Expectations:

Understanding and accepting that setbacks and challenges are a normal part of life is essential for resilience.

How to Implement:

- Regularly assess your goals and expectations. Ask yourself if they are realistic and achievable considering your current circumstances.
- Prepare mentally for the possibility of setbacks. Remind yourself that challenges don't signify failure but are natural parts of life's journey.
- When planning, factor in potential obstacles and think about how you would handle them.

b. Maintain a Positive Outlook:

A positive outlook can significantly impact your ability to handle stress and recover from setbacks.

How to Implement:

- Practice gratitude by acknowledging and appreciating the positive aspects of your life daily.
- Reframe negative experiences to focus on what they can teach you or how they can help you grow.
- Surround yourself with positive influences, including people, books, and media, to reinforce a hopeful perspective.

c. Solution-Focused Approach:

Adopting a solution-focused approach means directing your energy and efforts towards finding solutions rather than dwelling on problems.

How to Implement:

- When faced with a challenge, break it down into manageable parts and brainstorm possible solutions for each part.
- Focus on actions that you can control or influence rather than aspects beyond your control.
- Practice proactive problem-solving by anticipating potential challenges and planning how to address them.

d. Build a Support Network:

A strong support network of friends, family, and colleagues can provide emotional support and practical help during tough times.

How to Implement:

- Cultivate and maintain relationships with individuals who are supportive and understanding.
- Don't hesitate to reach out for help or advice when facing challenges.
- Participate in community groups or online forums where you can share experiences and learn from others.

e. **Develop Problem-Solving Skills:**

Enhancing your problem-solving skills can increase your confidence in handling difficulties, thereby boosting your resilience.

How to Implement:

- Engage in activities that challenge your problem-solving abilities, like puzzles, strategy games, or brain teasers.
- When faced with a problem, take a systematic approach: define the problem, generate potential solutions, evaluate these solutions, and then implement the best one.
- Reflect on past challenges and consider what strategies worked well for you. This reflection can help improve your problem-solving skills.

By proactively working on these strategies, you can build and fortify your resilience. This strength will not only help you navigate through current challenges but also prepare you for future obstacles, enabling you to lead a more fulfilling and less stressful life.

4. Empathy

Empathy is the emotional ability to understand and share the feelings of another. This emotional skill is key to forming deep, meaningful relationships. It allows you to connect with others on a profound level and to understand their perspectives, which is essential for emotional wellness and effective communication.

Practical Application: Enhancing Empathy

Empathy, the capacity to understand and share the feelings of others, is essential for building deep and meaningful connections. It involves more than just sympathizing with others; it's about genuinely stepping into their shoes and experiencing their emotions. Here are some practical ways to enhance your empathy:

a. Active Listening:

Active listening is about fully concentrating, understanding, responding, and then remembering what is being said. It's a central component of effective communication and empathy.

How to Implement:

- When someone is speaking, give them your full attention. Put aside distracting thoughts and avoid the urge to formulate your response while they are still talking.
- Observe the speaker's body language and tone of voice. Much of communication is nonverbal, and these cues can provide deeper insight into their feelings.
- Reflect back on what has been said by paraphrasing. "What I'm hearing is..." or "Sounds like you are saying..." are great ways to show that you are listening and understand.

b. Perspective-Taking:

Perspective-taking is the ability to see things from someone else's viewpoint. It involves putting aside your own thoughts and feelings to gain insight into another person's inner life.

How to Implement:

- Imagine yourself in the other person's situation. Ask yourself how you would feel and react if you were in their place.
- Consider the individual's background and experiences. Recognizing that their life experiences might differ from yours can help you better understand their perspective.
- Avoid making assumptions or jumping to conclusions. If unsure, ask the person to explain their viewpoint more fully.

c. Show Genuine Interest:

Showing genuine interest in others encourages them to open up and share more about their thoughts and feelings.

How to Implement:

- Ask open-ended questions that encourage the speaker to elaborate on their thoughts and feelings.
- Express curiosity and interest in their experiences. Phrases like "Tell me more about that" or "How did that make you feel?" can be encouraging.
- Be patient and give them time to respond. Avoid rushing the conversation or steering it back to yourself.

d. Practice Compassion:

Compassion involves recognizing a person's suffering and desiring to alleviate it. It's an essential aspect of empathy, especially in emotionally charged situations.

How to Implement:

- When someone is expressing difficult emotions, respond with kindness and understanding rather than judgment or solutions.
- Acknowledge their feelings, even if you don't fully understand or agree with them. Saying something like, "That sounds really tough, I'm here for you," can be comforting.
- Offer support and assistance. Sometimes, just being there for someone can be a powerful act of compassion.

By actively working on these aspects, you'll find that your ability to empathize with others improves significantly. Empathy enhances your relationships and enriches your understanding of the people around you, contributing to a more compassionate and connected world.

5. Optimism

Optimism is a mental attitude reflecting a belief or hope that the outcome of some specific endeavor, or outcomes in general, will be positive, favorable, and desirable. An optimistic mindset is associated with many benefits, including better health, higher levels of achievement, and greater overall happiness.

Practical Application: Cultivating an Optimistic Outlook

Optimism is not just about expecting the best to happen, but also about framing your mindset to view challenges in a more positive light. It involves an attitude of hope and confidence about the future or the successful outcome of something. Here's how you can nurture an optimistic outlook:

1. **Reframing Negative Thoughts:**

Reframing involves changing your perspective on a situation to view it in a more positive or productive light.

How to Implement:

- When you catch yourself having a negative thought, pause and assess its accuracy. Ask yourself, "Is there another way to look at this situation?"
- Actively challenge pessimistic thoughts. If you think, "This will never work," try to reframe it to, "I will find a way to overcome these challenges."
- Look for the learning opportunity or silver lining in difficult situations. This helps in shifting focus from what went wrong to what can be gained.

2. **Gratitude Practice:**

Practicing gratitude means regularly acknowledging the good in your life, which can significantly shift your perspective from lack to abundance.

How to Implement:

- Keep a gratitude journal. Each day, write down three things you are grateful for. These can be as simple as a sunny day or a good cup of coffee.
- Share your gratitude with others. This not only reinforces your positive feelings but can also improve the moods of those around you.

- Make it a habit to acknowledge and appreciate the small joys and successes in your daily life.

3. **Visualize Positive Outcomes:**

Visualization is the practice of creating a mental image of a future event. It helps in mentally preparing for a situation and fostering a positive outcome.

How to Implement:

- Take a few minutes each day to close your eyes and vividly imagine a scenario where you succeed in your goals.
- Picture yourself overcoming obstacles and achieving your desired outcome.
- Feel the emotions that come with success – joy, pride, satisfaction – to make the experience more powerful.

4. **Surround Yourself with Positive Influences:**

The environment and people around you can significantly influence your mood and outlook on life.

How to Implement:

- Spend time with people who uplift and support you. Positive relationships can increase your happiness and sense of well-being.
- Engage with positive media – books, movies, podcasts, etc., that inspire and motivate you.
- Avoid or limit exposure to negativity, whether it's from people, news, or social media.

By adopting these practices, you can develop a more optimistic outlook, which is a critical component of emotional wellness. Optimism not only improves your mental and emotional state but can also have positive effects on your physical health and overall life satisfaction.

Strategies for Developing Emotional Intelligence

Emotional Intelligence (EI) plays a crucial role in understanding and managing our own emotions and those of others. Here are detailed strategies to enhance your EI, along with practical solutions for incorporating them into daily life:

1. **Mindful Reflection:**

    Mindful reflection is about regularly examining your thoughts and feelings to understand your emotional processes.

    Practical Solutions:

    - **Daily Check-ins:** Set aside time each day, perhaps in the morning or before bed, to reflect on your emotions. Consider what you felt throughout the day, why you felt that way, and how you responded to those feelings.
    - **Emotion Journaling:** Keep a journal where you record your emotions and the events that triggered them. This can help in identifying patterns and understanding your typical emotional responses.
    - **Mindfulness Meditation:** Dedicate a few minutes each day to mindfulness meditation. Focus on your breath and observe your thoughts and feelings without judgment. This practice can improve your ability to recognize and understand your emotions as they occur.

2. **Active Listening:**

    Active listening is not just hearing but fully understanding and responding to what others are saying.

Practical Solutions:

- **Focused Attention:** When someone is speaking to you, give them your full attention. Put away distractions like phones or laptops.

- **Reflective Listening:** Repeat back what you've heard in your own words to show that you understand. For example, "It sounds like you're saying…" This not only confirms your understanding but also makes the speaker feel heard and validated.

- **Non-Verbal Cues:** Pay attention to the speaker's body language and tone, which can often convey more than words alone.

3. **Emotional Regulation:**

Managing intense emotions effectively is key to maintaining emotional balance.

Practical Solutions:

- **Deep Breathing Techniques:** When emotions run high, pause and take deep, slow breaths. This helps calm the nervous system and gives you time to process your feelings.

- **Mindfulness in Emotion:** Practice acknowledging your emotions without reacting immediately. Recognize what you're feeling and remind yourself that emotions are temporary.

- **Cognitive Restructuring:** Challenge negative thought patterns that arise during emotional times. Ask yourself if there's a more positive or realistic way to view the situation.

4. **Seek Feedback:**

Feedback from others can provide insights into your emotional tendencies and how they affect those around you.

Practical Solutions:

- **Feedback Sessions:** Ask close friends, family members, or trusted colleagues for honest feedback on how you handle emotions and interact with others.

- **360-Degree Feedback**: In a work setting, consider a 360-degree feedback process where you receive anonymous feedback from various people you interact with.

- **Reflect on Feedback:** Reflect on the feedback received without judgment. Use it as a learning tool to understand and improve your emotional interactions.

By integrating these strategies into your daily life, you can significantly enhance your emotional intelligence, leading to an improved relationship with yourself, better stress management, and a more fulfilling life. Remember, developing Emotional Intelligence is a journey, not a destination, and it requires continuous practice and commitment.

Linda's Transformation: From Self-Doubt to Self-Discovery

Linda's story is one of profound personal growth, illustrating the transformative journey from battling low self-esteem to embracing self-acceptance.

Linda, a graphic designer in her early thirties, had always struggled with feelings of inadequacy. Despite her talents and accomplishments, she was plagued by a persistent voice in her head that told her she wasn't good enough, smart enough, or worthy of happiness. This internal narrative led her down a path of self-criticism and depression, affecting her work, relationships, and overall quality of life.

Her journey towards self-acceptance began when she reached a breaking point. Realizing that her mental health was deteriorating, Linda sought the help of a therapist. This step marked the beginning of a transformative process that would gradually reshape her view of herself and her place in the world.

In therapy, Linda confronted the deep-seated beliefs that fueled her low self-esteem. She began to understand the origins of these beliefs, tracing them back to early life experiences. Her therapist guided her through the process of challenging and reframing these negative thoughts.

Simultaneously, Linda immersed herself in self-help literature. Books on personal growth, mindfulness, and self-compassion provided her with tools and insights that complemented her therapy sessions. She learned about the concept of self-talk and how her negative internal dialogue was impacting her self-esteem.

Linda began to practice positive self-talk. She would catch herself when she spiraled into negative thoughts and consciously replace them with affirmations of her worth and abilities. Phrases like "I am capable" and "I am worthy of happiness" became her mantras.

This practice of self-acceptance was not easy. It required her to be consistently mindful of her thoughts and reactions. However, over time, it became more natural. Linda noticed a significant shift in her mindset. She started to feel more confident in her skills and more comfortable in her own skin.

As Linda embraced self-acceptance, she found that her life began to change in positive ways. Her relationships improved as she interacted with others more openly and confidently. At work, she started to take on challenges that she would have previously shied away from, leading to career advancements and creative fulfillment.

Linda's journey from low self-esteem to self-acceptance is a testament to the power of personal transformation through self-awareness and intentional change. It's a story of how shifting one's internal dialogue can lead to profound improvements in one's sense of self and quality of life.

Now, equipped with a newfound understanding and acceptance of your emotions, it's time to step into the next phase of your journey. As we move forward, we'll explore the fundamental and often challenging realm of Stress Management. Here, we'll apply the insights and tools you've gained thus far to tackle one of life's most persistent hurdles. We'll discover strategies to not just cope with stress, but to master it, turning potential obstacles into stepping stones for growth and empowerment.

3. Stress Management – The Art of Staying Calm

As Benjamin Franklin wisely advised: *"Do not anticipate trouble, or worry about what may never happen. Keep in the sunlight."* - (Franklin)

Benjamin Franklin, one of the Founding Fathers of the United States, was not just a renowned politician but also a prolific writer, scientist, and inventor. His wisdom extends to various aspects of life, including personal well-being and stress management. In this quote, Franklin advises against excessive worry about future troubles, many of which may never come to pass.

Chapter 3: Stress Management – The Art of Staying Calm

Imagine standing in the eye of a storm, where all is calm and clear, while the world whirls chaotically around you. This is the art of stress management, the skill we embark on mastering in this chapter. Here, you'll learn not just to survive the storms of life but to stand resiliently at their center, unshaken and poised.

Stress, an inevitable companion in our journey through life, can either be a stumbling block or a stepping stone, depending on how we handle it. In this chapter, we turn what often feels like an insurmountable challenge into a manageable aspect of life. We will explore and equip you with a toolkit of techniques, each designed to help you navigate through stress with ease and confidence. From the tranquility of deep breathing exercises to the empowering practice of mindfulness and the rejuvenating power of physical movement, each strategy is a thread in the tapestry of stress resilience.

What Is Stress Management?

Stress management is an integral part of maintaining both mental and physical health. It's a misconception that stress management is solely about finding ways to relax or unwind after a stressful event. While relaxation is important, proper stress management is about cultivating a deeper, more resilient approach to the various challenges life presents. It involves developing a proactive mindset that empowers you to handle stressors with greater efficiency and less emotional upheaval.

At its core, stress management is about understanding that stress is an unavoidable aspect of life. Whether it's pressure at work, family responsibilities, or personal challenges, stress manifests in various forms and impacts everyone differently. Therefore, the art of staying calm is not about eliminating stress completely but about learning how to adapt to it, manage its intensity, and recover from its impacts effectively.

This approach to stress management requires a shift in perspective. It's about viewing stress not as a formidable enemy to be vanquished, but as a part of life that, when managed well, can lead to growth, resilience, and a deeper understanding of oneself. It involves recognizing the signals your body and mind give you when under stress and responding to these signals in a way that is both healthy and productive.

Developing this kind of resilience doesn't happen overnight. It requires practice, patience, and a willingness to explore various strategies that can help in mitigating the effects of stress. It's also about building a toolkit of resources – techniques, habits, and supports – that you can draw upon when faced with stressful situations.

Ultimately, the art of staying calm is a lifelong journey. It's an ongoing process of learning about yourself, understanding your unique stressors, experimenting with different coping mechanisms, and gradually building a robust, flexible approach to handling life's challenges. By committing to this journey, you not only improve your ability to manage stress but also enhance your overall quality of life.

Identifying and Understanding Your Stressors

Effectively managing stress begins with a clear understanding of what specifically triggers your stress response. Stressors are as unique as the individuals experiencing them and can range from external pressures like work deadlines and relationship issues to internal factors such as self-criticism or perfectionism.

Practical Approaches for Identification:

1. **Keep a Stress Diary:**

   - **How to Implement:** For the next one to two weeks, carry a small notebook with you or use a digital app to record instances where you feel stressed. Note the date, time, place, people involved, what you were doing, and how you felt both physically and emotionally.

   - **What to Look For:** Over time, look for patterns in your entries. Are there specific times of day, situations, or people that consistently trigger your stress? Do certain environments or activities tend to coincide with your stress response?

   - **Benefits:** This diary will serve as a tool to make you more aware of your stress triggers and help you understand the context in which they occur.

2. **Reflect on Your Responses:**

   - **How to Implement:** At the end of each day, spend a few minutes reflecting on the times you felt stressed. Pay attention to how your body reacted (tension, headache, stomach issues), what emotions you experienced (anger, sadness, frustration), and how you behaved (withdrawal, aggression, procrastination).

   - **What to Look For:** Identify any recurring physical symptoms or emotional patterns. Do you tend to react to stress with a particular set of emotions or behaviors?

   - **Benefits:** This reflection can help you become more attuned to your stress responses and develop more effective coping strategies.

3. **Seek External Input:**

   - **How to Implement:** Have open conversations with friends, family members, or colleagues. Ask them if they have noticed any patterns in your behavior that may indicate stress. Sometimes, others can see things that we might overlook.

- **What to Look For:** Pay attention to any observations they make about changes in your mood, behavior, or physical health that you may not have noticed.
- **Benefits**: This external perspective can provide valuable insights and reinforce or add to the findings from your stress diary and personal reflections.

Integrating the Findings into Your Life:

Once you have identified your primary stressors, you can begin to address them more effectively. The information gathered from your stress diary, reflections, and external input serves as a foundation for creating a personalized stress management plan. This plan might involve setting boundaries in personal relationships, developing new coping skills, changing your environment, or seeking professional support for deeper issues.

Understanding your stressors is not about eliminating stress entirely – which is often impossible – but about developing strategies to manage it effectively. By becoming more aware of what causes you stress and how you react to it, you can take proactive steps to reduce its impact on your life and wellbeing.

Effective Stress Reduction Techniques

After identifying your stressors, the next crucial step is to learn and apply effective techniques to manage and reduce stress. Since everyone responds differently to stress, it's important to find and tailor methods that resonate personally with you.

Practical Techniques for Stress Reduction:

1. **Deep Breathing Exercises:**
   - **How to Implement:** Practice diaphragmatic breathing by sitting comfortably or lying down, placing one hand on your abdomen, and taking slow, deep breaths. Focus on making your abdomen rise and fall, which indicates you're breathing deeply into your diaphragm.
   - **Frequency:** Integrate deep breathing into your daily routine, especially during moments of stress. Just a few minutes can be beneficial.
   - Benefits: Deep breathing stimulates the body's natural relaxation response, reducing stress hormone levels and inducing a state of calm.

2. **Mindfulness and Meditation:**
   - **How to Implement:** Allocate a few minutes each day for mindfulness or meditation. Find a quiet space, close your eyes, and focus on your breath or a simple mantra. Acknowledge wandering thoughts and gently bring your focus back.
   - **Variations:** Explore different forms of meditation, such as guided meditation, mindful walking, or body scan meditation, to see which suits you best.
   - **Benefits:** Regular practice can ground you in the present moment, diminish the impact of stress, and enhance overall emotional well-being.

3. **Physical Activity:**
   - **How to Implement:** Engage in physical activities that you enjoy. This could be a daily walk, a jog, a yoga session, or a dance class.
   - **Consistency:** Aim for regular physical activity, as consistency is key to reaping stress-relief benefits.
   - **Benefits**: Exercise releases endorphins, natural mood lifters, and can act as a form of meditation in motion, helping to clear and calm your mind.

4. **Relaxation Techniques:**

- **How to Implement:** Practice techniques like progressive muscle relaxation (tensing and relaxing muscle groups), guided imagery (visualizing a calm and peaceful setting), or enjoying a warm bath.

- **When to Use:** Utilize these techniques during your downtime or specifically when you feel stressed.

- **Benefits:** These practices promote relaxation of both the mind and body, helping to alleviate stress and induce a state of tranquility.

Building and Implementing a Comprehensive Personal Stress Management Plan

Creating a personal stress management plan involves a deliberate and thoughtful process of selecting and integrating strategies that resonate with you and address your specific stressors effectively. Here's a step-by-step guide to building a plan that is both practical and adaptable, ensuring it fits seamlessly into your life.

1. **Set Clear Goals:**

Identify Your Objectives: Start by clearly defining what you aim to achieve with your stress management plan. Goals can vary from reducing daily anxiety, improving sleep quality, to better handling work-related pressure.

Be Specific: The more specific your goals, the easier it will be to choose relevant techniques and measure your progress.

2. **Choose Techniques That Suit You:**

Reflect on Preferences: Based on insights from your stress diary and an understanding of different stress reduction techniques, select a few methods that you feel drawn to. This could be mindfulness meditation for mental clarity, physical activity for releasing tension, or relaxation techniques for better sleep.

Consider Your Lifestyle: Ensure the techniques you choose can be realistically integrated into your daily routine. For example, if you have a busy schedule, short mindfulness exercises throughout the day might be more feasible than long meditation sessions.

3. **Create a Routine:**

   - **Gradual Integration:** Slowly incorporate your chosen stress reduction techniques into your daily or weekly schedule. Start with one or two practices, and gradually build up as you become more comfortable.

   - **Set Reminders:** Use tools like alarms or scheduling apps to remind you to engage in your stress reduction activities. Consistency is key.

4. **Evaluate and Adjust:**

   - **Regular Reviews:** Periodically review the effectiveness of your stress management plan. Are you feeling more relaxed? Are you sleeping better? Is your work stress becoming more manageable?

   - **Be Flexible:** If certain techniques aren't working for you, don't hesitate to adjust your plan. Experiment with different methods until you find the right combination that works.

5. **Long-term Commitment:**

   - **Consistent Practice:** Understand that managing stress effectively requires ongoing effort. Make a commitment to consistently practice your chosen techniques.

   - **Mindset Shift:** Embrace stress management as a permanent part of your lifestyle, not just a temporary fix for stressful situations.

6. **Leverage Support Systems:**
    - **Seek Support:** Share your stress management goals with friends or family who can provide encouragement and accountability.
    - **Professional Guidance:** Consider seeking support from a therapist or coach, especially if you're dealing with chronic stress or anxiety.

By following these steps, you can develop a personalized stress management plan that not only helps you handle stress as it arises but also equips you with the tools to maintain a calm, centered state of being over the long term. Remember, the ultimate goal is not to eliminate stress completely but to cultivate a resilient, proactive mindset that allows you to navigate life's challenges with greater ease, balance, and confidence.

Resilience in the Fast Lane: Emily's Journey Through Stress

Emily's story is a powerful narrative of resilience and transformation.

As a dedicated project manager in a dynamic tech company, she faced immense pressure when tasked with leading a major project. With tight deadlines and a team relying on her guidance, Emily's world became a whirlwind of long hours and relentless dedication.

Initially, she believed that working harder was the key to success. However, this approach soon took its toll. Sleepless nights filled with worry became a norm, and her health began to decline, marked by frequent headaches and dwindling energy. The impact extended beyond her professional life, straining her personal relationships and leaving her emotionally drained.

The turning point came during a crucial presentation. Overwhelmed by anxiety, Emily had to step out, leaving her team bewildered. This incident was a wake-up call. It made her realize the need for change and led her to seek professional help.

In her journey to reclaim her life, Emily discovered the deep-rooted causes of her stress. Therapy sessions revealed her fear of failure and a tendency to ignore her own needs. She learned the importance of work-life balance and the need for self-care, leading her to set healthier boundaries at work and rediscover hobbies that brought her joy, like painting.

One significant change was the adoption of mindfulness meditation. This practice brought a sense of calmness and clarity to her mornings and transformed her approach to daily challenges.

The transformation was evident not just to Emily but to those around her. Her improved well-being positively influenced her professional and personal relationships. She became more than a manager to her team; she was a source of inspiration, embodying a leader who understood the importance of balance and mental health.

Emily's experience with stress led to profound personal growth. She emerged from this period of her life stronger and more resilient, with invaluable insights into managing stress and prioritizing well-being. Her story is a reminder that even in the depths of stress, there is a path to a more balanced and fulfilling life.

As we close the chapter on the art of staying calm amidst life's storms, you've equipped yourself with an arsenal of strategies to manage stress effectively. You've started to learn to stand resilient in the face of life's whirlwinds, finding calm in the chaos.

In this next chapter, we'll look into the heart of self-care. Here, we'll discover how treating ourselves with kindness, understanding, and forgiveness is not a luxury but a necessity. You'll learn practical ways to cultivate a compassionate inner voice, to be your own best friend in times of need, and to embrace your imperfections with open arms.

4: Self-Compassion – Being Kind to Yourself

"You yourself, as much as anybody in the entire universe, deserve your love and affection." – (Buddha)

This quote by Buddha, an eminent spiritual leader and founder of Buddhism, encapsulates the essence of self-compassion. His teachings often revolved around the importance of kindness, not only towards others but also towards oneself. In this simple yet profound statement, Buddha reminds us that self-love and self-compassion are not just acts of indulgence but are as essential as the love and compassion we extend to others.

Chapter 4: Self-Compassion – Being Kind to Yourself

Step into a space where the language is kindness, the atmosphere is understanding, and the ethos is unconditional self-love. Welcome to Chapter 4, a sanctuary where we learn the art of being kind to ourselves. In the hustle of daily life, where we often extend compassion to everyone but ourselves, this chapter serves as a gentle reminder of the importance of self-compassion.

Imagine embracing your imperfections not with criticism but with compassion. Picture a world where your self-talk is laced with encouragement and support, where every mistake is met with understanding, not judgment. This chapter is not just about concepts; it's about transforming the way you relate to yourself at the most fundamental level.

We'll explore practical, heartwarming strategies to cultivate a nurturing inner voice, to treat yourself with the patience and kindness you deserve, and to create an inner world as loving and forgiving as the one you wish to see around you. From mindful self-acceptance to the healing power of self-forgiveness, each page is a step towards a more compassionate relationship with yourself.

Understanding Self-Compassion

Understanding self-compassion involves a profound shift in the way we relate to ourselves, especially in times of difficulty or perceived failure. At its core, self-compassion is the practice of treating oneself with the same kindness, care and understanding that one would typically extend to a dear friend. It's rooted in the recognition that all humans are fallible and that making mistakes, experiencing setbacks, and having personal flaws are all inherent parts of the human condition.

Key Components of Self-Compassion:

- **Kindness vs. Judgment:** Self-compassion requires us to be gentle with ourselves. Where we might usually respond to our errors or shortcomings with harsh self-criticism, self-compassion invites us to respond with kindness and understanding. This shift in perspective involves speaking to ourselves in a supportive and warm manner, just as we would console a friend who is going through a tough time.

- **Common Humanity vs. Isolation:** Often, when we encounter personal failings, we feel as though we are the only ones suffering or making mistakes. However, self-compassion involves recognizing that suffering, failure, and imperfection are part of the shared human experience. Everyone goes through difficult times; everyone faces challenges. This awareness helps us feel more connected to others in our struggles rather than feeling isolated and alienated.

- **Mindfulness vs. Over-Identification**: Self-compassion involves a balanced approach to our negative emotions. Mindfulness, a key component of self-compassion, allows us to observe our painful feelings with openness and clarity without over-identifying with them. It means acknowledging our emotions without letting them define us or sweep us away. This mindful awareness creates a space where we can view our situation with a greater perspective and respond to our pain with compassion rather than getting lost in our emotional reactions.

Practical Implications of Self-Compassion:

In practice, cultivating self-compassion can have profound effects on our overall well-being. When we start treating ourselves with compassion, we begin to develop a more supportive and loving relationship with ourselves. This nurturing attitude can lead to increased resilience, a decrease in anxiety and depression, and a more balanced emotional life. We become better equipped to handle life's challenges because we're not adding the extra layer of self-criticism to our existing problems.

Moreover, self-compassion fosters a sense of inner peace and contentment as we learn to accept ourselves, flaws and all. It encourages us to be more forgiving and less judgmental of ourselves, leading to a healthier state of mind. We start to recognize that our worth is not contingent on our successes and failures but is inherent in our very being.

In essence, understanding and practicing self-compassion means embarking on a journey towards a more compassionate, accepting, and kinder way of being with ourselves. It's about building an inner sanctuary of peace and kindness that supports us through life's ups and downs.

Six Practical Ways to Cultivate Self-Compassion

1. **Mindful Acknowledgment of Suffering:**

    Under the umbrella of cultivating self-compassion, "Mindful Acknowledgment of Suffering" plays a pivotal role. This practice revolves around the conscious recognition and acceptance of one's feelings, particularly during challenging times or when encountering negative self-talk. It's a fundamental shift from a typical instinctive reaction – often a mix of avoidance, denial, or harsh self-judgment – towards a more accepting and nurturing approach to one's emotional state.

    a. **Understanding Mindful Acknowledgment:**

        *   **Recognizing Emotional States:** The first step in mindful acknowledgment is to become aware of your emotional responses. This might mean noticing feelings of frustration, sadness, anxiety, or any other form of emotional discomfort. The key is to observe these

feelings without immediately trying to suppress or rationalize them away.

- **Pausing and Reflecting:** Once you recognize these emotions, the next step is to pause. This pause is crucial; it's a deliberate break from the automaticity of habitual reactions. In this pause, you give yourself the space to process what you're feeling.

- **Validating Your Feelings:** Validation is an essential component of this process. It involves acknowledging that your feelings are valid, regardless of the circumstances that elicited them. Phrases like "This is a tough moment" or "It's okay to feel this way" are affirmations that what you're experiencing is real and acceptable. It's a form of giving yourself permission to feel without judgment.

b. **The Practice and Its Benefits:**

To practice mindful acknowledgment of suffering, you can incorporate the following steps into your daily routine:

- **Routine Check-ins:** Regularly check in with yourself throughout the day. Ask yourself how you're feeling and acknowledge any discomfort or emotional pain that arises.

- **Journaling:** Writing about your emotions can provide a deeper understanding and validation. It's a tangible way to acknowledge and process your feelings.

- **Self-Compassion Reminders:** Place reminders in your environment to pause and practice self-compassion. These could be notes, alerts on your phone, or visual cues that remind you to check in with yourself.

- **Breath as an Anchor:** Use your breath as a tool to center yourself when you're feeling overwhelmed. Focus on breathing slowly and deeply, which can help calm the mind and make it easier to acknowledge and process your emotions.

The benefit of this practice lies in its ability to transform our relationship with our emotions. By acknowledging and validating our feelings, we move away from a cycle of self-criticism and towards a more compassionate understanding of our emotional experiences. This shift not only enhances our emotional well-being but also fosters a more accepting and nurturing inner dialogue. In the long run, the practice of mindful acknowledgment can lead to greater emotional resilience, self-awareness, and a more profound sense of inner peace.

2. Self-Compassion Breaks:

In the realm of cultivating self-compassion, the concept of "Self-Compassion Breaks" is a powerful tool, especially during moments of stress or overwhelm. This practice is about intentionally creating a space of kindness and understanding for oneself in the midst of challenging situations.

a. The Essence of Self-Compassion Breaks:

- **Acknowledging the Need for a Break:** The first step is to recognize when you are experiencing stress or emotional turmoil. This awareness is crucial for initiating a self-compassion break. It's about giving yourself permission to pause and attend to your well-being.

- **Finding a Quiet Space:** Once you've acknowledged your need for a break, the next step is to find a quiet and comfortable space where you can be undisturbed for a few minutes. This space doesn't have to be physically large; it can be a small corner in your office, a park bench, or even just closing your eyes at your desk.

- **Deep Breathing for Calmness:** Deep breathing is a simple yet effective way to calm the nervous system. By taking slow, deep breaths, you signal your body to relax, creating a serene foundation for your self-compassion break. Focus on breathing in slowly, holding for a moment, and then exhaling longer than your inhale.

- **Offering Comforting Words:** Speak to yourself with comforting, supportive words. Phrases like "I'm going through a hard time right now, but I'm here for myself" serve as affirmations of self-support. These words are a verbal embrace, acknowledging your current state and offering yourself kindness and understanding.

b. **Implementing Self-Compassion Breaks:**

To effectively implement self-compassion breaks in your daily routine, consider the following:

- **Prompt Yourself:** Set reminders on your phone or computer to take regular self-compassion breaks, especially during known stressful periods.

- **Script Your Self-Compassion Phrases:** Prepare a few go-to phrases that resonate with you. These can be words of encouragement, understanding, or validation.

- **Mindful Awareness:** During your break, try to be fully present in the moment. If your mind wanders, gently bring it back to your breathing and the comforting words you're offering yourself.

- **Physical Comfort:** If possible, engage in a physical gesture of comfort, like placing a hand over your heart or giving yourself a gentle hug. Physical touch can reinforce the feeling of self-compassion.

c. Benefits of Self-Compassion Breaks:

Self-compassion breaks are more than just a momentary pause; they offer numerous benefits:

- **Reduced Stress:** By acknowledging and addressing stress in the moment, these breaks can prevent stress from escalating.
- **Increased Resilience:** Regular self-compassion breaks build emotional resilience, as they teach you to handle difficult emotions with grace and understanding.
- **Improved Self-Relationship:** These breaks strengthen your relationship with yourself, fostering a sense of self-trust and -care.

In essence, self-compassion breaks are a vital practice in the journey of self-care. They allow you to honor your emotions and provide yourself with the same care and attention that you would offer to a loved one, reinforcing a nurturing and supportive inner environment.

3. Challenge Negative Self-Talk:

Challenging negative self-talk is a crucial aspect of practicing self-compassion. It involves being mindful of the tone and content of your internal dialogues and actively working to transform them into more positive, supportive narratives.

a. Understanding Negative Self-Talk:

Negative self-talk often manifests as a critical inner voice that can be harsh, demeaning, or downright abusive. This voice might echo past criticisms from others or stem from internalized negative beliefs about oneself. Common examples include thoughts like "I'm not good enough," "I can't do anything right," or "I don't deserve happiness."

b. **Steps to Challenge Negative Self-Talk:**

- **Recognition:** The first step is to become aware of your negative self-talk. Often, these thoughts are so ingrained that they go unnoticed. Begin by paying attention to your thoughts, especially during times of stress or when facing challenges.

- **Pause and Reflect:** When you catch yourself engaging in negative self-talk, pause. Take a moment to acknowledge these thoughts. Ask yourself, "Is this thought helpful? Is it kind?" This pause is crucial for breaking the automatic cycle of negativity.

- **Reframe Your Thoughts:** Once you've identified negative self-talk, actively work on reframing these thoughts in a more compassionate and realistic way. For example, if you find yourself thinking, "I'm such a failure," challenge this by thinking, "I made a mistake, but I can learn from this." This reframing should acknowledge the situation realistically but also offer kindness and the possibility for growth.

- **Develop Compassionate Responses:** Create a list of compassionate responses and affirmations that you can turn to when you notice negative self-talk. These can be general affirmations like "I am doing my best, and that's enough," or specific responses tailored to frequent negative thoughts you experience.

c. **Implementing the Practice in Daily Life:**

To make this practice a part of your daily life, consider the following:

- **Journaling:** Keep a journal where you record instances of negative self-talk and how you reframed them. This can help you track your progress and notice patterns in your thinking.

- **Reminders:** Place reminders in your environment to practice positive self-talk. These could be notes, phone wallpapers, or stickers with affirmations.

- **Mindfulness Meditation:** Engage in mindfulness meditation focused on observing your thoughts. This practice can help you become more aware of your internal monologue and provide the space to change it.

d. **Benefits of Challenging Negative Self-Talk:**

- **Improved Mental Health:** Reducing negative self-talk can lead to decreased levels of stress, anxiety, and depression.

- **Increased Self-Esteem:** As you become kinder to yourself, your self-esteem and self-confidence can improve.

- **Better Decision-Making:** With a more positive internal dialogue, you're likely to make choices that are more in line with your true needs and values.

Challenging negative self-talk is not about denying your feelings or experiences but about approaching them with understanding and kindness. This shift in how you talk to yourself can have a profound impact on your overall well-being and outlook on life.

4. **Write a Compassionate Letter to Yourself:**

Writing a compassionate letter to yourself is an effective and therapeutic self-compassion practice. It involves penning a letter to yourself with the same kindness, understanding, and encouragement that you would offer to a dear friend facing challenges.

a. **Steps to Write a Compassionate Letter:**

- **Set the Tone: Approach** this exercise with an open heart and a non-judgmental mindset. Imagine you're writing to a close friend who is experiencing the challenges and feelings you are facing.

- **Acknowledge Your Challenges:** Begin by openly acknowledging the specific challenges and difficulties you are currently experiencing. Describe them as you would in a conversation with a friend, without self-criticism or minimization.

- **Validate Your Feelings:** Express understanding and validation for your feelings. It's important to convey that it's okay to feel the way you do and that your emotions are valid and understandable, given your circumstances.

- **Offer Words of Comfort and Encouragement:** Provide yourself with words of comfort. These can include affirmations, reassurances, or reminders of your strengths and past accomplishments. Write encouraging statements that uplift and bolster your spirit.

- **End with Hope and Positivity:** Conclude the letter with a message of hope and optimism. Express belief in your ability to navigate through the current challenges and affirm that things can and will get better.

b. **Implementing the Practice in Daily Life:**

- **Choose a Quiet Time**: Select a quiet and comfortable time to write your letter, free from distractions and interruptions.

- **Handwrite the Letter:** If possible, handwrite the letter. The physical act of writing can be a more emotionally connected and therapeutic process.

- **Read It When Needed:** Keep the letter in a place where you can access it easily. Read it whenever you find yourself being overly critical or harsh towards yourself. The words you wrote during a moment of compassion can provide comfort and perspective during more challenging times.

c. **Benefits of Writing a Compassionate Letter:**

- **Emotional Release:** Writing the letter can be a cathartic experience, allowing you to express and process emotions that you might not have fully acknowledged.

- **Increased Self-Compassion:** This exercise can help reinforce a more compassionate and understanding relationship with yourself.

- **Perspective Shift**: Reading the letter later can provide a shift in perspective, reminding you to treat yourself with the same kindness you would offer to others.

Writing a compassionate letter to yourself is a simple yet powerful way to cultivate self-kindness and to remind yourself of your worth, especially during times of self-doubt or criticism. It reinforces the understanding that you deserve the same compassion and empathy that you so readily give to others.

Example Letter

Olivia is a 50-year-old veterinarian who has been feeling overwhelmed with work pressures and struggling with self-doubt. Here's an example of a compassionate letter Olivia might write to herself:

Dear Olivia,

I'm writing this letter to you, not just as yourself but as a friend who truly understands and cares. I see the challenges you're facing lately, especially at work, where the pressure seems unending. I know you're doing your best, and that's more than enough.

Remember last week when you worked late to attend to that emergency case? That showed incredible dedication. But Olivia, it's also okay to take breaks. It's okay not to be perfect. You are human, and humans need rest and moments of peace. Please don't be hard on yourself for needing the same.

I've noticed you've been doubting your skills, wondering if you're really good enough. Let me remind you of the expertise and compassion that I, and everyone else, see in your veterinary care. Your work isn't just skilled; it's heartfelt. It's you. And 'you' is someone incredibly special.

It's alright to feel overwhelmed sometimes. It doesn't make you weak; it makes you real. But amidst these challenging moments, don't forget your strength, resilience, and the times you've overcome similar situations. You have a track record of rising above, and I believe in you to do it again.

Please be kind to yourself. Treat yourself with the same compassion and understanding you so generously give to your patients. You deserve that kindness, too. Remember, taking care of yourself isn't selfish; it's necessary. You are worthy of every moment of peace and happiness.

On the days when self-doubt creeps in, remember this letter. Remember that you are valued, skilled, and more than capable. The journey might be rough at times, but I have no doubt you'll navigate it beautifully. You always do.

With all the love and support in the world,

Olivia

5. Develop a Self-Compassion Mantra:

Developing a self-compassion mantra is a powerful practice for fostering a kinder, more supportive relationship with oneself. This mantra serves as a personal affirmation—a short, positive phrase that you can repeat to yourself, particularly during moments of stress, self-criticism, or emotional difficulty.

a. **Creating Your Self-Compassion Mantra:**

- **Choose Words That Resonate:** Your mantra should be personal and meaningful to you. It could address an aspect of self-compassion you're working on, like self-acceptance or kindness. Phrases like "I am worthy of kindness" or "I am a work in progress, and that's okay" are good examples. The key is to choose words that resonate deeply with you and reflect the kind of self-compassion you need.

- **Keep It Simple and Positive:** A mantra is most effective when it is concise and positively framed. It should be easy to remember and recite. The simplicity of the mantra helps it become a grounding tool that can be used in various situations.

- **Alignment with Your Values:** Ensure that your mantra aligns with your core values and the person you aspire to be. This alignment makes the mantra more powerful as it echoes your deeper beliefs and aspirations.

b. **Implementing the Mantra Practice:**

- **Regular Repetition:** Incorporate your mantra into your daily routine. Repeat it to yourself each morning, night, or during meditation sessions. The more you repeat your mantra, the more ingrained it becomes in your mindset.

- **Use in Challenging Times:** Whenever you find yourself grappling with negative thoughts or feelings, pause and repeat your mantra. It can be a helpful tool to shift your focus from self-criticism to self-compassion.

- **Combine with Breathwork:** Pair your mantra with deep, mindful breathing for added calming effect. Breathe in as you silently say your mantra, and breathe out any tension or negativity.
- **Reminder Cues:** Place reminders of your mantra around you. This could be a note on your mirror, a wallpaper on your phone, or a small card in your wallet. These cues can prompt you to practice your mantra throughout the day.

c. **Benefits of a Self-Compassion Mantra:**

- **Reduces Negative Self-Talk**: Regularly repeating a self-compassion mantra helps counteract patterns of negative or critical self-talk, gradually replacing them with more positive, nurturing messages.
- **Increases Resilience:** By reinforcing a compassionate mindset, a mantra can help you navigate difficult situations more calmly and with greater emotional resilience.
- **Enhances Self-Awareness:** This practice increases mindfulness and self-awareness, as it encourages you to pause and reflect on your inner state.
- **Promotes Emotional Well-Being:** Over time, the use of a self-compassion mantra can lead to increased feelings of self-worth, acceptance, and overall emotional well-being.

In essence, a self-compassion mantra is more than just a phrase; it's a tool for nurturing a more compassionate and forgiving relationship with yourself. Through its regular practice, you can cultivate a kinder inner dialogue, leading to a more balanced and emotionally healthy life.

Helpful Mantra Examples:

Each of these mantras is designed to reinforce positive self-perception, encourage self-acceptance, and foster a nurturing attitude towards oneself. You can choose one or several that resonate with you and incorporate them into your daily routine to cultivate self-compassion.

1. "I am worthy of kindness and respect."
2. "I am enough, just as I am."
3. "I embrace my strengths and my flaws."
4. "I choose to treat myself with compassion."
5. "I deserve love and happiness."
6. "Mistakes are part of learning and growing."
7. "I am a work in progress, and that's perfectly okay."
8. "I am patient with myself as I evolve."
9. "My feelings are valid and important."
10. "I allow myself the space to heal and grow."
11. "I am capable of overcoming challenges."
12. "I treat myself with the same kindness I give to others."
13. "I am deserving of self-care and rest."
14. "I forgive myself and learn from my experiences."
15. "I am strong, resilient, and brave."
16. "Every day, I grow stronger and more compassionate."
17. "I release judgment and embrace acceptance."
18. "I am gentle with myself in moments of struggle."
19. "I honor my journey and its unique pace."
20. "I am surrounded by love and support."

6. Practice Gratitude for Yourself:

Practicing gratitude for oneself is an essential component of self-compassion and overall well-being. This practice involves regularly recognizing and appreciating your own positive qualities, efforts, and achievements. It's about shifting focus from what you perceive as lacking or flawed within yourself to acknowledging and valuing your strengths and contributions.

a. **Understanding Self-Gratitude:**

- **Acknowledging Positive Qualities:** Self-gratitude starts with recognizing your positive attributes. This could be your kindness, creativity, work ethic, sense of humor, or any other quality you value in yourself. It's about seeing and appreciating the good within you.

- **Appreciating Your Efforts and Achievements:** Often, we overlook the effort we put into our daily lives, whether in professional settings, personal projects, or relationships. Practicing gratitude for yourself means acknowledging both your big and small achievements, as well as the effort behind them, even if the outcomes weren't as expected.

- **Recognizing Personal Growth:** Acknowledge the ways you've grown over time. This can include improvements in skills, emotional maturity, knowledge, or how you handle certain situations. It's important to celebrate your journey and progress.

b. **Implementing Self-Gratitude Practices:**

- **Gratitude Journaling:** One effective way to practice self-gratitude is through keeping a gratitude journal. Dedicate a few minutes each day to write down things about yourself that you are grateful for. This could include achievements of the day, qualities you appreciate about yourself, or moments where you felt proud of your actions.

- **Daily Affirmations:** Incorporate affirmations into your routine that focus on gratitude towards yourself. Phrases like "I am grateful for my resilience" or "I appreciate my ability to learn and grow" can be powerful.

- **Reflection Time:** Set aside time regularly to reflect on your accomplishments and growth. This could be a quiet moment at the end of each day, week, or month.

- **Celebrating Successes:** Celebrate your successes, no matter how small they may seem. This could be treating yourself to something special or simply taking a moment to acknowledge and savor your success.

c.   **Benefits of Practicing Self-Gratitude:**

- **Improved Self-Esteem:** Regularly practicing gratitude towards yourself can lead to an improved sense of self-worth and self-esteem.

- **Increased Positivity:** Focusing on the positive aspects of yourself can shift your overall outlook to be more optimistic.

- **Reduced Negative Self-Talk:** By acknowledging your positive traits and achievements, you can counteract tendencies towards negative self-talk and self-criticism.

- **Enhanced Well-Being:** Studies have shown that gratitude practices are linked to greater well-being, happiness, and physical health.

Practicing gratitude for oneself is a powerful way to nurture a positive and compassionate relationship with yourself. It encourages a balanced view of oneself, where you're not solely defined by your shortcomings or challenges but also by your strengths, efforts, and the unique qualities that make you who you are.

By incorporating these practices into your daily life, you'll gradually cultivate a more compassionate relationship with yourself. This shift towards self-compassion can lead to improved mental well-being, reduced stress and anxiety, and a more fulfilling and balanced life. Remember, being kind to yourself is not a luxury but a vital component of your overall health and happiness.

As we conclude our journey through the nurturing landscapes of self-compassion, where we've learned the art of being kind and understanding towards ourselves, we stand at the threshold of a new yet intrinsically connected realm: the realm of holistic health. In Chapter 4, we embraced the power of self-compassion, learning how our inner dialogue shapes our emotional well-being. We discovered that the way we treat ourselves mentally and emotionally has profound effects on our overall sense of self.

Now, as we step into Chapter 5, 'Holistic Health – The Mind-Body Connection,' we expand our exploration to understand how this inner kindness and emotional wellness are deeply intertwined with our physical health. This next chapter takes us deeper into the philosophy that our bodies and minds are not separate, isolated entities but are instead parts of a complex, interconnected system.

In the upcoming pages, we'll uncover the symbiotic relationship between mental and physical well-being. We'll explore how our thoughts, emotions, and attitudes can directly influence our physical health and, conversely, how our physical state can impact our mental and emotional landscape. From the food we eat to the way we move, sleep, and even breathe, every aspect of our lifestyle contributes to this holistic picture of health.

We'd Love to Hear Your Thoughts So Far!

Dear Reader,

As you transition from pages of Chapter 4 to the new horizons of Chapter 5, we warmly invite you to take a brief pause. This is a special moment – a chance for you to share your reflections and insights, which are not only valuable to us but immensely helpful to others on similar paths of self-discovery and personal growth.

How has this journey been for you up until now? Have the initial chapters ignited a spark within you, brought about a shift in perspective, or provided a haven of tranquility? Your shared experiences and feedback don't just enrich our understanding – they light the way for fellow readers. Your unique perspective offers encouragement, inspiration, and a sense of camaraderie to those who walk this path alongside you, even if in silence.

We kindly ask you to spare a moment to leave a review. Express your thoughts, emotions, and any personal transformations you've encountered thus far. Remember, your voice is incredibly powerful – it can uplift, motivate, and foster a sense of community, where collective wisdom and mutual support thrive.

Thank you for being an essential part of this shared journey. Your contribution is invaluable, and we eagerly anticipate hearing from you.

Love it? Leave a Review

With Heartfelt Gratitude,

Eliza Bennet & Inspire Self Growth Publishing

5: Holistic Health – The Mind-Body Connection

"Every cell in your body is eavesdropping on your thoughts."

(Deepak Chopra)

Deepak Chopra is a prominent figure in the field of mind-body medicine and holistic health. An Indian-American author, public speaker, and alternative medicine advocate, Chopra has gained widespread recognition for his contributions to discussions about wellness, spirituality, and mind-body healing. He has authored numerous books that blend elements of traditional Eastern wisdom with modern science, particularly in areas like meditation, consciousness, and holistic health.

https://www.deepakchopra.com/

Chapter 5: Holistic Health – The Mind-Body Connection

Welcome to a journey where every breath links your mind to your body, and every thought weaves into the fabric of your health. Chapter 5, 'Holistic Health – The Mind-Body Connection,' opens the door to a realm where the physical and the mental are not just connected but are expressions of each other. Here, we will unravel the mystery of how a serene mind can lead to a vibrant body and how our physical well-being can elevate our mental space.

Imagine a world where your mental stress can manifest as physical symptoms and where physical exercise can elevate your mood and mental clarity. This chapter isn't just about understanding these connections; it's about harnessing them to create a balanced, healthier you. Get ready to explore transformative practices that unite body and mind and to hear inspiring stories of real-life transformations.

Your journey to holistic health starts here, a journey that redefines what it means to be truly well.

Exploring the Mind-Body Link

The concept of the mind-body link is at the heart of holistic health. It suggests a profound and intricate connection between our psychological state and our physical well-being. This isn't merely a philosophical notion; it's a reality backed by an ever-growing body of scientific research. Understanding this link is essential for anyone looking to improve their overall health and quality of life.

The Science of the Mind-Body Connection

- **Impact of Mental Stress on Physical Health:**
  - Chronic stress is more than just a psychological issue. It triggers a series of physiological responses, like the release of stress hormones (cortisol

and adrenaline), which in the short term are part of the body's natural fight-or-flight response. However, when these responses are continuously activated, they can lead to health problems such as high blood pressure, heart disease, and a weakened immune system.

- o Stress can also contribute to the development of conditions like obesity, type 2 diabetes, and gastrointestinal disorders. Prolonged stress affects digestion, metabolism, and even how the body processes fat, leading to these conditions.

- **Physical Activity and Mental Health:**
  - o Exercise is a well-documented mood booster. When you engage in physical activity, your body releases endorphins, often known as 'feel-good' hormones. These natural mood lifters play a significant role in reducing anxiety and depression.
  - o Regular physical activity has been shown to improve cognitive function, enhance memory and concentration, and even stimulate the growth of new brain cells. It's a powerful tool for overall mental wellness.

- **Benefits of Positive Mental Health Practices:**
  - o Practices like meditation, mindfulness, and yoga don't just calm the mind; they have tangible benefits for the body. For instance, meditation has been shown to lower blood pressure, improve heart rate, and boost the immune system.
  - o Mindfulness and relaxation techniques can reduce the production of stress hormones, thereby mitigating their harmful effects on the body.

Putting the Mind-Body Connection into Practice

- **Mindful Stress Management:** Incorporate stress management techniques such as deep breathing, meditation, or yoga into your daily routine. These practices help calm the mind, which in turn can have a positive impact on your physical health.

- **Regular Physical Activity:** Engage in regular physical activities like walking, jogging, swimming, or any form of exercise you enjoy. Physical activity not only improves your physical health but also supports your mental well-being.

- **Balanced Diet:** Eating a balanced diet plays a critical role in both physical and mental health. Nutrient-rich foods can improve brain function, energy levels, and overall body health.

- **Adequate Sleep:** Prioritize getting enough sleep. Quality sleep is crucial for both mental clarity and physical health. It helps in the repair and rejuvenation of the body and mind.

- **Reflective Journaling:** Keep a journal to reflect on your mental state and how it affects your physical health. This can help you become more aware of the mind-body link in your own life.

- **Professional Guidance:** Consider seeking advice from healthcare professionals who specialize in integrative medicine. They can provide guidance tailored to your unique mind-body needs.

By understanding and harnessing the mind-body link, you can take significant strides toward improving your overall health. This connection highlights the importance of treating both mental and physical health not as separate entities but as interconnected components of your total well-being. With this knowledge, you are empowered to make lifestyle choices that foster both mental peace and physical vitality.

Integrative Approaches to Holistic Health

Holistic health transcends the traditional view of treating just the symptoms of illness. It's a comprehensive approach that considers the entire spectrum of a person's life – physical, emotional, mental, and spiritual. By integrating various methods, holistic health promotes overall well-being and vitality. This section will guide you through several integrative practices that combine traditional medical treatments with alternative therapies and lifestyle adjustments.

1. Yoga: A Union of Body, Mind, and Breath

Yoga is more than just physical exercise; it's a practice that balances body, mind, and spirit. It combines physical postures (asanas) with controlled breathing and meditation.

Practicing yoga regularly can lead to significant improvements in flexibility, strength, balance, and endurance. On a mental level, it helps in reducing stress, anxiety, and depression, enhancing overall mental clarity and peace.

To integrate yoga into your life, start with beginner-friendly classes or online tutorials. Pay attention to how different postures and breathing techniques affect your mental and physical state.

2. Acupuncture: Balancing the Body's Energy

Acupuncture, a key component of traditional Chinese medicine, involves inserting thin needles into specific points on the body. It's based on the principle of balancing the body's energy flow (Qi).

It's used to treat a variety of physical and mental health issues, including chronic pain, anxiety, insomnia, and migraines.

If you're new to acupuncture, seek a licensed practitioner who can explain the process and customize treatments to your specific needs.

3. Nutrition and Mental Health

Diet plays a crucial role in both physical and mental health. Certain foods can significantly affect mood, energy levels, and cognitive function.

Incorporate foods rich in omega-3 fatty acids, antioxidants, vitamins, and minerals to support brain health. Examples include fatty fish, nuts, seeds, fruits, and vegetables.

Consider consulting a nutritionist who can provide personalized dietary advice based on your health goals and needs.

4. Integrating Conventional and Alternative Therapies

Holistic health doesn't dismiss conventional medicine. Instead, it advocates for a complementary approach, where traditional medical treatments are used alongside alternative therapies.

If you're undergoing medical treatment, discuss with your healthcare provider how you can safely incorporate holistic practices to support your treatment.

5. Lifestyle Adjustments for Well-Being

Small changes in your daily routine can have a significant impact on your overall health. This includes regular physical activity, adequate sleep, stress management techniques, and making time for hobbies and activities you enjoy.

Reflect on your current lifestyle and identify areas where you can introduce healthier habits.

Embracing integrative approaches to holistic health means recognizing the interconnectedness of all aspects of your being. By combining different methods of care, you can achieve a more balanced and harmonious state of health. Remember, holistic health is a journey of continuous exploration and adjustment, aiming for a state of well-being that encompasses your entire being – body, mind, and spirit.

Reclaiming Wellness: Emma's Victory Over Stress and Pain

Let me share a story about someone I once knew, who we'll call 'Emma.' Emma's journey is a testament to the transformative power of holistic health and the mind-body connection.

"Emma, in her early forties, was a software developer, a job that demanded long hours in front of a computer. Over time, she began experiencing chronic back pain and frequent migraines. These physical ailments soon started affecting her mental health, leading to stress and anxiety. The more stressed she became, the worse her physical symptoms seemed to get. It was a vicious cycle that left Emma feeling helpless and exhausted.

Realizing she needed a change, Emma began exploring holistic health practices. She started with yoga, initially seeking relief for her back pain. But what she found was much more. The physical postures, combined with deep breathing and meditation, not only alleviated her pain but also brought a sense of calm and clarity to her mind.

Encouraged by these changes, Emma delved deeper into holistic health. She adjusted her diet, incorporating more nutrient-rich foods that boosted her energy levels and improved her mood. She also began regular acupuncture sessions, which helped in reducing her migraines and enhancing her overall sense of well-being.

But the most significant change came in Emma's approach to her work-life balance. She became more mindful of her time, ensuring she took breaks and engaged in activities that brought her joy and relaxation. She started spending weekends hiking and reconnecting with nature, which brought her a deep sense of peace and groundedness.

Over the course of a year, the transformation was remarkable. Emma's back pain and migraines became infrequent, and her stress levels significantly reduced. She reported feeling more vibrant, both physically and mentally, than she had in years. Her journey beautifully illustrates how holistic health practices can create a harmonious mind-body connection, leading to profound changes in one's health and quality of life.

Emma's story is a powerful reminder that our mental and physical health are deeply interconnected. By addressing both with a holistic approach, we can find balance and healing in ways that traditional methods alone may not achieve."

As we close this enlightening chapter on the synergistic dance between mind and body, we're equipped with a deeper understanding of holistic health and the tools to harness this powerful connection. The journey ahead leads us into the empowering world of Personal Growth – Embracing Change. In the next chapter, we build on the foundation of holistic health to explore how embracing and navigating life's changes can lead to profound personal development and well-being.

6: Personal Growth – Embracing Change

"To improve is to change; to be perfect is to change often." –

(Churchill)

Sir Winston Churchill was a prominent figure in 20th-century British politics. He served as the Prime Minister of the United Kingdom during crucial periods, including World War II, where his leadership and determination played a pivotal role in the Allied victory. Churchill was known for his eloquent speeches and writings, making him a respected orator and statesman. This quote highlights the importance of embracing change as a means of personal growth and continuous improvement, which can be particularly relevant in both professional and personal contexts.

Chapter 6: Personal Growth – Embracing Change

Step into the world of transformation where change is not just inevitable but a golden key to unlocking your true potential. Welcome to Chapter 6, 'Personal Growth – Embracing Change.' Here, we journey through the dynamic landscape of personal development, where change becomes the catalyst for growth, self-discovery, and profound transformation.

Imagine if the challenges and obstacles you face were actually stepping stones, guiding you towards realizing your dreams and uncovering strengths you never knew you had. In this chapter, we will look into the art of setting meaningful goals, not just any goals, but those that resonate with your deepest aspirations and propel you forward.

But setting goals is just the beginning. We'll explore the resilience and tenacity required to overcome obstacles and how these challenges are critical for your personal growth. Embracing change isn't just about adapting; it's about actively shaping your journey, turning every hurdle into an opportunity for learning and every setback into a lesson in strength.

And to truly bring this message home, you'll be inspired by real-life stories of personal transformation. These are not tales of unattainable feats but honest accounts of individuals who, just like you, navigated the winds of change and emerged stronger, wiser, and more fulfilled.

So, are you ready to embark on this transformative journey? Are you prepared to embrace change, not with apprehension, but with anticipation and excitement for what lies ahead? Turn the page, and let's begin the journey of embracing change and fostering personal growth together.

Setting Goals for Personal Development

Embarking on a journey of personal growth begins with setting clear and meaningful goals. Goals give direction, focus, and a sense of purpose. But how do you set goals that not only inspire but are also achievable and aligned with your personal development? Let's break down this process into clear, actionable steps:

1. **Reflect on Your Values and Aspirations:**

   Start by reflecting on what truly matters to you. What are your core values? What aspects of your life do you want to improve or change? This could be your health, career, relationships, or personal skills.

2. **Define Specific and Measurable Goals:**

   Instead of vague goals like "be healthier" or "be more successful," define specific and measurable objectives. For instance, "run a 5K in three months" or "complete a professional certification in six months."

3. **Ensure Your Goals are Attainable and Relevant:**

   While it's good to be ambitious, your goals should be realistically achievable. They should also be relevant to your long-term aspirations. Ask yourself, "Is this goal feasible with my current resources and time?" and "Does this goal help me move closer to where I want to be?"

4. **Set Short-Term Milestones:**

   Break down your larger goals into smaller, manageable tasks or milestones. This step-by-step approach keeps you motivated and makes your goals less daunting.

5. **Create a Timeline:**

   Assign a clear timeline for each goal and milestone. Deadlines create a sense of urgency and help you manage your time effectively.

6. **Write Down Your Goals:**

   Document your goals in writing. This act reinforces your commitment and helps you remember and reflect on your goals.

7. **Regular Review and Adjustments:**

   Life is unpredictable, and flexibility is vital. Regularly review your goals and be willing to make adjustments as needed. This could mean extending a deadline or modifying a goal in light of new circumstances.

8. **Seek Support and Accountability:**

   Share your goals with a trusted friend, family member, or mentor. They can provide support advice, and hold you accountable.

9. **Celebrate Progress:**

   Acknowledge and celebrate your progress, no matter how small. This practice builds confidence and keeps you motivated.

10. **Reflect and Learn:**

   Regularly reflect on your journey. What's working? What challenges are you facing? Use these reflections to learn and grow.

Practical Application:

Now, let's put this into practice. Take a moment to write down one goal you'd like to achieve in the next six months. Follow the steps outlined above to refine this goal, break it down into milestones, and create a timeline. Keep this goal in a visible place and revisit it regularly. Remember, the journey to achieving your goals is as important as the destination. Embrace each step, learn from the challenges, and allow yourself to grow and evolve through the process.

As we embark on the path of personal development, setting clear and achievable goals is crucial. But often, the process can seem daunting or abstract. Let's walk through a real-life example to bring it into a more concrete perspective. This will not only illustrate how to effectively set and pursue a goal but also provide a relatable blueprint that you can apply to your own aspirations. Meet 'Alex', who has set a goal to learn a new language. By following Alex's journey, you'll gain valuable insights into transforming your own goals from mere ideas into achievable realities.

Example Goal: Learning a New Language - Spanish

Initial Goal: Imagine someone named 'Alex', who has always wanted to learn Spanish. Alex's initial goal is: "I want to learn Spanish."

1. **Reflect on Values and Aspirations:** Alex values cultural diversity and loves traveling. Learning Spanish aligns with these values and aspirations.

2. **Define Specific and Measurable Goals:** Alex refines the goal to: "Achieve conversational fluency in Spanish in six months."

3. **Ensure Goals are Attainable and Relevant:** Alex assesses the goal against current commitments and resources. The goal is challenging but attainable and relevant to Alex's love for travel.

4. **Set Short-Term Milestones:**

   - **Milestone 1:** Complete an online beginner's course in Spanish in two months.

- **Milestone 2:** Practice with a language partner once a week for three months.
- **Milestone 3:** Engage in 30 minutes of Spanish conversation daily in the last month.

5. **Create a Timeline:** Alex sets specific dates for completing each milestone, spreading them evenly over the six-month period.

6. **Write Down the Goal:** Alex writes down the refined goal and milestones in a journal.

7. **Regular Review and Adjustments:** Alex decides to review progress every two weeks, adjusting the plan as needed based on learning pace and other life commitments.

8. **Seek Support and Accountability:** Alex joins a language learning group and informs a close friend about the goal for support and accountability.

9. **Celebrate Progress:** After completing the beginner's course, Alex celebrates by having a dinner at a Spanish restaurant.

10. **Reflect and Learn:** Throughout the process, Alex regularly reflects on what's working well (like using language apps) and challenges (like finding enough time for practice).

Practical Application for Readers:

Now, take a leaf from Alex's book. Think about a goal you want to achieve. It could be anything from improving your physical fitness to learning a new skill or improving a personal relationship. Follow the same steps Alex did:

- Define your goal clearly.
- Make sure it aligns with your values.
- Break it down into achievable milestones.
- Set a timeline.
- Write it down and review it regularly.

- Seek support and be ready to adjust your plan as you go.

- Most importantly, remember to celebrate your progress and learn from the journey.

This methodical approach not only makes your goal more attainable but also turns the process into a rewarding journey of personal growth.

Overcoming Obstacles and Embracing Growth

Embarking on a journey of personal development is a path filled with inevitable challenges. These obstacles, whether external, like time constraints and lack of resources, or internal, such as fear, self-doubt, and limiting beliefs, are integral parts of the growth and change process. However, it's how we approach and navigate these obstacles that can profoundly impact our personal development journey.

1. **Identifying and Acknowledging Obstacles:**

   Start by identifying these challenges and acknowledging them without judgment. Understand that they are not barriers to your success but rather opportunities for growth and learning. This perspective is crucial, as it transforms potentially discouraging situations into moments ripe for problem-solving and personal evolution. Remember, true growth often happens outside of your comfort zones, so embrace the discomfort as an indicator of your development.

2. **Developing a Problem-Solving Mindset:**

   When facing these obstacles, adopt a problem-solving mindset. Break down the issues into smaller, more manageable parts and brainstorm creative solutions. It's essential to remain open and flexible, as sometimes the most effective solutions are not the most obvious ones.

3. **Seeking Support and Creating an Action Plan:**

Don't hesitate to seek support from mentors, peers, or professionals. Others can offer valuable perspectives and encouragement. Once you've identified potential solutions, develop a clear action plan with steps and deadlines to overcome each obstacle. Be prepared to adjust this plan as necessary, staying flexible and adaptable.

4. **Maintaining a Growth Mindset and Persistence:**

A key to overcoming obstacles is maintaining a growth mindset. Believe in your ability to learn and improve from each challenge. View feedback and criticism as opportunities for growth, not as reflections of your worth. Stay committed and persistent in your goals, even when progress seems slow. Small, consistent steps can lead to significant change over time.

5. **Celebrating Progress and Reflecting on the Journey:**

Regularly celebrate your achievements, no matter how small. This not only boosts your morale but reinforces your commitment to personal growth. Reflect on your journey periodically, evaluating what you've learned and how you've grown. This reflection is incredibly motivating and insightful.

6. **Adjusting Goals and Incorporating Growth into Daily Life:**

As you grow and evolve, be open to adjusting your goals. This flexibility allows you to embrace new opportunities and insights as they arise. For example, if you've successfully incorporated regular workouts into your routine, consider setting a new goal, like participating in a run or exploring a different exercise form.

Embracing growth through overcoming obstacles is a lifelong process. Each challenge faced is an opportunity to learn more about yourself, develop new skills, and become a more well-rounded individual. Keep pushing forward, embracing each new challenge with curiosity and courage, and continue growing into the best version of yourself. Your journey is a powerful testament to your resilience and determination, a journey that transforms challenges into stepping stones for success and personal fulfilment.

Inspirational Stories of Personal Transformation

Rachael's Story:

Rachael, an interior designer in her early forties, faced a turning point when her company decided to downsize. The news came as a shock, leaving her in a whirlpool of uncertainty and worry about her future. Accustomed to a stable routine, Rachael initially saw this change as a derailment of her career and life plans.

However, as she began embracing change, a new perspective began to take root. Rachael realized that this change could be an opportunity to reassess her career and personal aspirations. She started by identifying her main obstacle: fear of stepping out of her comfort zone.

Embracing a new mindset, Rachael began viewing the situation not as a setback but as a chance for growth and exploration. She set out to redefine her career goals, aligning them more closely with her passion for environmental activism. She broke down her broader goal of career transition into smaller, actionable steps, starting with enrolling in a course on sustainable design.

Rachael sought support from peers and mentors who encouraged her to pursue her passion. She crafted a detailed action plan, setting timelines for completing her course, building a portfolio in sustainable design, and networking within the industry.

Each step forward bolstered Rachael's confidence. She celebrated small milestones, like completing a challenging project or making a new professional connection. These moments of acknowledgment fueled her journey, reinforcing her belief in her capabilities.

Reflecting on the process, Rachael marveled at her evolution. From the uncertainty and fear, she had emerged more focused, skilled, and aligned with her true passions. Her resilience paid off when she landed a role in a prestigious firm specializing in eco-friendly design projects.

Rachael's story beautifully encapsulates the essence of embracing personal growth and navigating change. Her journey from trepidation to triumph is a vivid example of how challenges can be transformed into opportunities for learning, growth, and fulfillment. Rachael's renaissance is a reminder to us all that embracing change, though daunting, can open doors to new possibilities and lead us to discover strengths we never knew we had. Let her story inspire and encourage you to view life's twists and turns not as obstacles but as pathways to a richer, more fulfilling life.

Fiona's Story:

Fiona, a school administrator in her late fifties, found herself at a crossroads when she felt an overwhelming sense of stagnation in her career. While secure, her job no longer brought her the satisfaction it once did. She yearned for something more, something that aligned with her growing interest in holistic health and wellness.

Initially, Fiona was hesitant to make any changes due to the risks involved. She had a stable job, and the idea of venturing into a new field seemed daunting. However, as she read about embracing change for personal growth, Fiona began to see this period in her life not as a crisis but as an opportunity for exploration and self-discovery.

She started by identifying her primary obstacle: the fear of the unknown and potential financial instability. Addressing these fears head-on, Fiona began to explore her options. She started attending workshops and seminars on holistic health during her free time, gradually immersing herself in a community that shared her passion.

Fiona set clear, achievable goals. Her first goal was to gain a certification in nutritional therapy. She meticulously planned out her steps, balancing her current job responsibilities with her studies. She reached out to professionals in the field, seeking guidance and mentorship, which provided her with invaluable insights and encouragement.

As Fiona progressed in her studies, her confidence grew. Each small achievement was a cause for celebration, reinforcing her belief in her path. She began to share her knowledge with friends and family, which not only bolstered her confidence but also honed her skills.

Eventually, Fiona reached a pivotal moment when she felt ready to transition fully into her new career. The journey was not without its challenges, but her resilience, planning, and passion kept her steadfast. Her leap of faith paid off when she successfully transitioned into a role as a holistic health consultant, a role that filled her with a sense of purpose and joy that she had not felt in years.

Fiona's story is a powerful testament to the transformative impact of embracing change and pursuing personal growth. Her journey from a state of career stagnation to finding her passion and purpose in holistic health is a vivid illustration of how stepping out of one's comfort zone can lead to profound fulfillment and success. Fiona's story serves as an inspiring reminder that it's never too late to reassess our paths and chart new courses towards a life that resonates with our deepest passions and aspirations. Let her story motivate you to embrace your own journey of growth and change with courage and an open heart.

As we conclude Chapter 6, 'Personal Growth – Embracing Change,' we reflect on the inspiring journeys of individuals like Fiona and Rachael, who have shown us the transformative power of embracing change. Their stories highlight that change, while inevitable, is a potent catalyst for personal development. It's a call to step out of our comfort zones, confront our fears, and grow resilient. Remember, your path of personal growth is unique. Let the principles and strategies we've discussed guide you as you navigate the waters of change, embracing each new experience with an open heart and mind.

Yet, as we journey through change and personal growth, we must not lose sight of our mental health. It's the foundation upon which our ability to adapt and thrive rests. As we transition into the next chapter, 'Mental Health – Prioritizing Your Psychological Well-Being,' we'll delve into the importance of nurturing our mental and emotional states. This chapter will offer strategies to maintain and improve mental health, understand stress management, and build resilience. It's about thriving mentally and emotionally, recognizing that caring for our mind is essential for a fulfilling life journey. Let's continue this transformative journey, embracing not only the changes in our lives but also prioritizing the well-being of our minds and hearts.

7: Mental Health – Prioritizing Your Psychological Well-Being

"The greatest weapon against stress is our ability to choose one thought over another." – (James)

William James was a pioneering American psychologist and philosopher, often referred to as the "Father of American psychology." Born in 1842, James made significant contributions to the fields of psychology, philosophy, and education. He is best known for his influential works, such as "The Principles of Psychology," which laid the groundwork for many future theories in psychology, including the functionalist theory. James was a strong advocate for the importance of individual experience and the power of the human mind.

Chapter 7: Mental Health – Prioritizing Your Psychological Well-Being

Pause for a moment and consider this startling fact: according to the World Health Organization, one in four people in the world will be affected by mental or neurological disorders at some point in their lives. Yet, despite its prevalence, mental health often remains shrouded in silence and stigma. This is your invitation to a journey deep into the realm of mental health, a journey that is not just enlightening but also crucial.

In our fast-paced, high-stress world, prioritizing psychological well-being is more important than ever. Imagine navigating life's complexities not just with physical vigor but with a mind fortified by resilience, clarity, and balance. In the following pages, we explore the intricate relationship between our thoughts, emotions, and behaviors, unraveling the complexities of mental health.

Envision a life where effectively managing stress, anxiety, and other mental challenges is a reality within your grasp. Think of a world where emotional resilience is your fortress, enabling you to face life's ups and downs with courage and poise.

We're not just exploring theories and concepts but equipping you with practical tools and strategies to enhance your mental well-being. This is about empowering you to take control of your mental health to build a life marked by emotional strength and psychological balance.

Are you ready to take this vital step towards understanding and nurturing your mental health? Let's embark on this journey together, uncovering the power and potential of our mental landscapes.

Five Common Mental Health Challenges and Solutions

Mental health challenges are a part of the human experience, affecting individuals across all walks of life. Understanding these challenges and knowing how to address them is vital for maintaining psychological well-being. Let's explore some common mental health issues and practical, empathetic solutions to help manage them.

1. **Anxiety and Stress:**

    Challenge: Anxiety and stress are pervasive issues, often characterized by feelings of tension, worried thoughts, and physical changes like increased blood pressure.

    Solution: Mindfulness and relaxation techniques are effective in managing anxiety. Practices like deep breathing, meditation, and yoga can help calm the mind. Additionally, regular physical activity and a balanced diet play a significant role in reducing symptoms.

2. **Depression:**

    Challenge: Depression is a mood disorder marked by persistent feelings of sadness, loss of interest, and a range of emotional and physical problems.

    Solution: Seek professional help as a primary step. Engage in regular exercise and maintain a routine to bring structure to your day. Activities like journaling and practicing gratitude can also be beneficial. Social support is essential, so stay connected with friends and family.

3. **Sleep Disorders:**

Challenge: Common sleep disorders include insomnia, sleep apnea, and restless leg syndrome, leading to poor sleep quality and affecting overall health.

Solution: Establish a regular sleep routine, create a comfortable sleep environment, and limit exposure to screens before bedtime. Mindfulness and relaxation techniques before bed can also be helpful. If problems persist, consult a healthcare provider.

4. **Substance Abuse:**

Challenge: Substance abuse refers to the harmful use of substances, including alcohol and drugs, leading to addiction and other health issues.

Solution: Professional counseling and rehabilitation programs are critical for recovery. Support groups can provide community and accountability. Engaging in healthy activities and building a solid support network are also vital components of recovery.

5. **Eating Disorders:**

Challenge: Eating disorders, including anorexia, bulimia, and binge-eating disorder, are serious conditions that affect both physical and mental health.

Solution: Professional treatment is essential. Cognitive-behavioral therapy (CBT) and nutritional counseling can be effective. It's also important to develop a healthy relationship with food and body image, which can be supported through therapy and support groups.

Implementing Solutions with Empathy and Understanding:

- **Seek Professional Help:** For all mental health challenges, seeking help from a qualified professional is essential. They can provide a proper diagnosis and tailored treatment plan.

- **Build a Support Network:** Surround yourself with people who understand and support you. This network can include friends, family, support groups, or a mental health professional.

- **Practice Self-Care:** Regular exercise, a balanced diet, adequate sleep, and time for relaxation and hobbies are vital components of mental health.

- **Stay Informed:** Educate yourself about your condition. Understanding what you're facing can empower you to take control of your health.

Dealing with mental health challenges requires patience, understanding, and persistence. Remember, it's a journey of small steps, and each step forward is a victory. Be kind to yourself, celebrate your progress, and know that with the right tools and support, positive change is not just possible but within your reach. Let this guide be a starting point for a journey towards a healthier, happier you.

Eight Techniques for Maintaining Positive Mental Health

Maintaining positive mental health is essential for a fulfilling and balanced life. It involves proactive steps and practices that contribute to overall psychological well-being. Here's a detailed guide on various techniques that are practical, easy to follow, and can be implemented by anyone to maintain and enhance mental health.

1. **Mindfulness and Meditation:**

Technique: Regular practice of mindfulness and meditation can significantly improve mental clarity and reduce stress. It involves focusing on the present moment and observing thoughts and sensations without judgment.

Implementation: Start with just a few minutes a day, using guided meditation apps or videos if you're a beginner. Gradually increase the duration over time.

2. **Regular Physical Exercise:**

Technique: Exercise is not just good for the body but also for the mind. It releases endorphins, known as 'feel-good' hormones, which can improve mood and reduce feelings of anxiety and depression.

Implementation: Incorporate at least 30 minutes of moderate exercise into your daily routine. This could be brisk walking, cycling, yoga, or any physical activity you enjoy.

3. **Balanced Diet and Nutrition:**

Technique: A balanced diet that includes essential nutrients can have a positive impact on your mental health. Certain foods, like those rich in omega-3 fatty acids, can enhance brain function and mood.

Implementation: Include a variety of fruits, vegetables, lean proteins, and whole grains in your diet. Stay hydrated and limit the intake of caffeine and sugar.

4. **Adequate Sleep:**

Technique: Quality sleep is crucial for mental health. It helps the brain to rest and recharge, improving cognitive function and emotional regulation.

Implementation: Aim for 7-9 hours of sleep each night. Establish a regular sleep schedule and create a restful environment free from distractions like electronic devices.

5. **Social Connections:**

Technique: Building and maintaining healthy social connections can provide emotional support and reduce feelings of loneliness and isolation.

Implementation: Regularly connect with friends and family, whether it's through in-person meetings, phone calls, or social media. Participate in community or group activities that interest you.

6. **Stress Management:**

Technique: Effective stress management is key to maintaining mental health. Techniques include deep breathing, relaxation exercises, and time management.

Implementation: Identify your stress triggers and develop coping strategies—practice relaxation techniques like deep breathing or progressive muscle relaxation.

7. **Hobbies and Interests:**

Technique: Engaging in hobbies and activities that you enjoy can provide a sense of achievement and relaxation.

Implementation: Dedicate time each week to a hobby or interest that brings you joy, whether it's reading, gardening, painting, or any other activity.

8. **Positive Thinking:**

   Technique: Cultivating a positive mindset can influence your overall mental health. This involves practicing gratitude, positive self-talk, and optimism.

   Implementation: Keep a gratitude journal, challenge negative thoughts with positive ones, and focus on the good aspects of your life.

Implementing these techniques requires commitment and consistency, but the benefits to your mental health are immeasurable. Remember, maintaining positive mental health is an ongoing process. Be patient with yourself, and recognize that it's okay to have ups and downs. Each step you take towards caring for your mental well-being is a step towards a happier and healthier you.

Resources and Support Systems

As we navigate the complexities of mental health, it's important to remember that reaching out for help is not just a sign of strength but a vital step towards well-being. Whether you're facing challenges with anxiety, depression, stress, or any other mental health issue, know that support is available and accessible. The resources and support systems listed below offer a range of services across the US, Canada, UK, Europe, and Australia, designed to provide guidance, understanding, and care.

Here is a list of some main resources and support systems available in various regions, providing a starting point for anyone seeking help and support in their mental health journey.

United States:

1. **National Alliance on Mental Illness (NAMI): Website: nami.org**
   Offers support, education, advocacy, and public awareness so that individuals and families affected by mental illness can build better lives.

2. **Substance Abuse and Mental Health Services Administration (SAMHSA): Helpline: 1-800-662-HELP (4357) Website: samhsa.gov**

   Provides information on mental health treatment and resources and has a helpline for immediate assistance.

3. **Mental Health America (MHA): Website: mhanational.org**

   Focuses on prevention, early identification, intervention for those at risk, and integrated care.

Canada:

1. **Canadian Mental Health Association (CMHA): Website: cmha.ca**

   Offers a range of mental health services and supports across Canada.

2. **Bell Let's Talk: Website: letstalk.bell.ca**

   Promotes mental health awareness and support across Canada.

3. **Wellness Together Canada: Website: wellnesstogether.ca**

   Provides free online resources, tools, apps, and connections to trained volunteers and qualified mental health professionals.

United Kingdom:

1. **Mind: Website: mind.org.uk**

   Provides advice and support to empower anyone experiencing a mental health problem.

2. **NHS Mental Health Services: Website: nhs.uk**

   Offers access to a range of mental health services, including counseling and psychotherapy.

3. **Samaritans: Helpline: 116 123 (UK and ROI) Website: samaritans.org**

   Available 24/7 for anyone who needs someone to talk to.

Europe:

1. **Mental Health Europe (MHE): Website: mhe-sme.org**

Represents associations, organizations, and individuals committed to the promotion of positive mental health.

2. **European Alliance for Mental Health - Employment & Work (EUMH Alliance): Website: eumhalliance.com**

   Focuses on mental health in the workplace.

Australia:

1. **Beyond Blue: Website: beyondblue.org.au**

   Provides information and support to help everyone in Australia achieve their best possible mental health.

2. **Black Dog Institute: Website: blackdoginstitute.org.au**

   Offers clinical resources, digital tools, and apps focused on mood disorders.

3. **Lifeline Australia: Helpline: 13 11 14 Website: lifeline.org.au**

   A national charity providing all Australians experiencing emotional distress with access to 24-hour crisis support and suicide prevention services.

These resources provide various forms of support, from helplines and therapy to educational materials and advocacy. It's important to seek help when needed and know that there are numerous avenues for support and guidance in mental health matters.

Closing Chapter 7 on 'Mental Health,' we've gained knowledge and tools to navigate its complexities, emphasizing the importance of seeking help when needed. Now, in Chapter 8, 'Self-Love – Your Path to Inner Peace,' we focus on cultivating self-compassion. Exploring the transformative power of self-love, we'll see how it positively impacts every aspect of life, fostering inner contentment and enduring peace. Join me on this enlightening journey towards self-love, fundamental for a content, peaceful, and happy life.

8: Self-Love – Your Path to Inner Peace

"Love yourself first and everything else falls into line. You really have to love yourself to get anything done in this world." - (Dyer)

Dr. Wayne Dyer was a prominent self-help author and speaker known for his works on personal development and spiritual growth. He believed in the transformative power of self-love and emphasized its significance in achieving success and fulfillment. In this quote, Dr. Dyer underscores the idea that self-love is the foundation upon which all other aspects of life can be built. When you prioritize and love yourself, it becomes easier to navigate challenges, pursue your goals, and find inner peace.

https://www.drwaynedyer.com/

Chapter 8: Self-Love – Your Path to Inner Peace

Imagine a world where the first person you truly fall in love with is yourself. This is not a journey of vanity or self-obsession but a profound voyage into the heart of self-compassion and acceptance. Welcome to a vital chapter in your journey of personal growth: 'Self-Love – Your Path to Inner Peace.'

In a society that often pushes us towards relentless self-improvement, the concept of self-love can seem foreign, even indulgent. Yet, it is the very essence of a fulfilled and peaceful life. Self-love is about understanding and embracing who you are, flaws and all. It's about treating yourself with the same kindness and understanding you generously offer to others.

This chapter isn't just about feeling good about yourself; it's about creating a foundation of inner peace that influences every aspect of your life. It's about breaking free from the chains of self-criticism and doubt and stepping into a space where you acknowledge and appreciate your own worth.

As we explore the depths of self-love, you'll discover how this powerful practice can transform your mindset, relationships, and overall well-being. You'll learn practical strategies to cultivate self-love and how it can be the key to unlocking a life of contentment and joy.

The Importance of Self-Love

At the core of our well-being, happiness, and life satisfaction lies a concept that is often overlooked yet fundamentally transformative – self-love. This profound practice goes far beyond mere self-care or self-esteem; it is about cultivating a deep-seated acceptance and appreciation for oneself. Let's explore the multifaceted importance of self-love in an engaging and enlightening way.

1. **Foundation of Mental and Emotional Health:**
   - Self-love is vital for mental and emotional health. It fosters a positive self-image and helps combat negative emotions and thoughts. When you love and accept yourself, you are less likely to fall into the trap of negative self-talk and more likely to handle emotional challenges with resilience.
   - It also acts as a buffer against stress, anxiety, and depression. By recognizing your own worth, you build a protective barrier that can shield you from the impact of external pressures and criticisms.

2. **Enhances Relationships:**
   - Self-love directly impacts the quality of your relationships. When you value yourself, you set the standard for how you expect to be treated by others. This leads to healthier, more fulfilling relationships, as you are likely to choose partners who respect and value you as much as you do yourself.
   - It also prevents dependency on others for validation and happiness, creating a more balanced dynamic in relationships. Loving yourself teaches you to love others better, fostering empathy and understanding.

3. **Decision Making and Boundaries:**
   - With self-love comes the clarity and strength to make better decisions for yourself. You become more attuned to your needs and desires, enabling you to make choices that align with your true self.
   - It also empowers you to set and maintain healthy boundaries. When you understand your worth, you are less likely to tolerate disrespect or mistreatment, whether in personal or professional contexts.

4. **Motivation and Personal Growth:**
   - Self-love is a powerful motivator. When you believe in your own value, you are more driven to pursue your goals and dreams. It fuels your

ambition and provides the courage to face challenges and embrace opportunities for growth.

- It encourages a mindset of growth and learning, where mistakes and failures are seen as valuable lessons rather than reflections of your worth.

5. Overall Life Satisfaction:

- Self-love leads to a deeper sense of contentment and satisfaction with life. It allows you to appreciate your journey, celebrate your achievements, and find joy in the present moment.

- This inner contentment radiates outward, affecting all areas of your life, from your career to your relationships to your physical health.

In essence, self-love is the cornerstone of a fulfilling, well-rounded life. It's about embracing your uniqueness, acknowledging your worth, and treating yourself with kindness and respect. By cultivating self-love, you not only enhance your own life but also enrich the lives of those around you. Embrace this journey of self-love and watch as it transforms your world, bringing more joy, peace, and fulfillment into every aspect of your life.

Seven Steps to Cultivate a Loving Relationship with Yourself

Cultivating a loving relationship with yourself is a journey that can lead to profound self-discovery and fulfillment. It involves practices and mindsets that nurture self-compassion, self-acceptance, and self-respect. Here are some engaging and practical steps to build a more loving relationship with yourself, designed to be easy to understand and implement in your daily life.

1. Begin with Self-Acceptance:

Practice: Start by accepting yourself as you are, with all your imperfections and strengths. Understand that being imperfect is part of being human.

Implementation: Each morning, look in the mirror and affirm, "I accept myself as I am today." Acknowledge your strengths and areas for growth without judgment.

2. **Set Aside Time for Self-Reflection:**

Practice: Regular self-reflection helps in understanding your thoughts, feelings, and behaviors.

Implementation: Dedicate a few minutes each day to reflect on your experiences. Use a journal to write down your thoughts, emotions, and learnings.

3. **Engage in Activities You Love:**

Practice: Doing things you enjoy can significantly boost your mood and self-esteem.

Implementation: Make a list of activities that bring you joy and make time for at least one of these activities every day. It could be as simple as reading, gardening, or listening to your favorite music.

4. **Practice Mindfulness:**

Practice: Mindfulness helps you stay grounded in the present moment and develop a deeper understanding of yourself.

Implementation: Try mindfulness exercises like deep breathing, mindful walking, or meditation. Even a few minutes a day can be beneficial.

5. **Develop Positive Self-Talk:**

Practice: The way you talk to yourself matters. Cultivate a positive and encouraging internal dialogue.

Implementation: Notice when you engage in negative self-talk and consciously replace those thoughts with positive affirmations. Phrases like "I am capable" or "I am worthy" can be powerful.

6. **Take Care of Your Physical Health:**

Practice: Physical health is closely linked to mental health. Taking care of your body is a form of self-love.

Implementation: Maintain a healthy diet, exercise regularly, and ensure adequate rest and sleep.

7. **Set Boundaries:**

Practice: Setting healthy boundaries is crucial for self-respect and self-love.**Implementation:** Learn to say no to things that drain your energy or go against your values. Communicate your needs and limits to others clearly.

Building a loving relationship with yourself is not an overnight process but a continuous journey of self-discovery and care. By implementing these steps, you can create a foundation of self-love that enhances every aspect of your life. Remember, the relationship you have with yourself sets the tone for all other relationships in your life. Nurture it with kindness, patience, and understanding, and watch as it transforms your world, bringing more happiness, confidence, and inner peace.

Transforming Self-Doubt into Self-Acceptance

A critical aspect of our journey towards self-love and inner peace involves transforming self-doubt into self-acceptance. This transformation extends beyond merely overcoming negative thoughts; it represents a profound shift in our self-perception and the way we treat ourselves at the deepest level. Embracing self-acceptance is about changing the narrative we tell ourselves, moving from a place of self-criticism to one of understanding and compassion. It's a fundamental change that impacts not just how we think but how we feel and act in our daily lives, paving the way for a more harmonious and contented existence.

Understanding Self-Doubt:

Self-doubt often stems from internalized messages and beliefs that we've picked up over the years, whether from family, society, or personal experiences. It manifests as a critical inner voice that questions our abilities, worth, and decisions. This voice can be paralyzing, leading to indecision, anxiety, and a lack of self-trust.

The Eight-Step Journey to Self-Acceptance:

Transforming self-doubt into self-acceptance is a journey that requires patience, effort, and, often, a change in perspective.

1. **Recognize and Challenge the Inner Critic:** Begin by becoming aware of your inner critic. Notice when self-doubt creeps in and how it affects your emotions and behaviors.

2. **Challenge these thoughts.** Ask yourself, "Is this thought based on facts or my own perceptions?" "Would I say this to someone I care about?" Often, you'll find that these doubts are not reflections of reality but rather harsh self-judgments.

3. **Reframe Your Thoughts:** Practice reframing your thoughts. Replace self-doubt with affirmations that reinforce your abilities and worth. For instance, change "I can't do this" to "I can do this, and I can learn from the challenges."

4. **Cultivate Self-Compassion:** Treat yourself with the same kindness and understanding you would offer a friend. When you fail or make a mistake,

instead of beating yourself up, offer words of comfort and encouragement to yourself.

5. **Celebrate Your Strengths and Successes:** Regularly acknowledge and celebrate your strengths and successes, no matter how small they may seem. This practice helps to build confidence and diminish self-doubt.

6. **Embrace Imperfection:** Understand that imperfection is part of the human experience. Accepting that you can't be perfect in everything frees you from the unrealistic expectations that fuel self-doubt.

7. **Seek Support When Needed:** Sometimes, self-doubt can be overwhelming, and it's okay to seek support. This could be from friends, family, mentors, or mental health professionals.

8. **Implementing Self-Acceptance:** Incorporate these practices into your daily routine. For example, start your day with a positive affirmation, keep a journal where you note down successes and strengths, and practice mindfulness to stay present and connected with yourself.

As we embrace our journey from self-doubt to self-acceptance, fostering peace, confidence, and inner harmony, we naturally progress to the next crucial step: integrating self-care into our daily lives. This next section will guide us in embedding practical self-care routines, enriching our journey towards a deeper and more fulfilling relationship with ourselves.

9: Implementing Self-Care in Daily Life

"Self-care is not selfish. You cannot serve from an empty vessel." – (Brownn)

Eleanor Brownn is a popular self-help author known for her writings on self-care and personal development. Her works have inspired countless individuals to prioritize self-care in their lives.

Chapter 9: Implementing Self-Care in Daily Life

In a world where the relentless pace of life can leave us feeling overwhelmed and depleted, the concept of self-care emerges as a radiant beacon of hope and healing. It's a practice that transcends boundaries, a universal remedy embraced by individuals from all walks of life. From the profound wisdom of celebrated authors to the illuminating insights of influential activists and spiritual leaders, the significance of self-care resonates deeply within us.

As we venture into the heart of Chapter 9, titled "Implementing Self-Care in Daily Life," we embark on a transformative journey guided by the profound words of those who have not only spoken of self-compassion but have lived its principles. Within these pages, we will explore the remarkable power of self-care and discover how it can seamlessly weave into the tapestry of our daily existence.

Together, we will unlock the secrets to nurturing our physical, emotional, and mental well-being. Through the profound insights and practical strategies shared by these revered individuals, you'll find the tools to craft a life imbued with self-compassion and resilience.

Creating a Sustainable Self-Care Routine

Establishing a sustainable self-care routine is about integrating practices into your daily life that nourish and rejuvenate you, both mentally and physically. It's not about grand gestures but about small, consistent acts that collectively make a significant impact on your well-being. Here's a guide to creating a self-care routine that is both sustainable and personally enriching.

1. Assess Your Needs:

To build a self-care routine that truly works for you, it's essential to start by assessing your needs. Consider these steps:

- Take some time to reflect on different aspects of your life, such as physical health, mental well-being, emotional stability, and overall happiness.

- Identify areas where you feel you need improvement or more attention. This might include finding ways to manage stress, improve your physical fitness, or boost your mental clarity.

- Pay attention to activities or practices that genuinely make you feel good and bring you joy. It could be something as simple as a daily walk, spending time with loved ones, or engaging in a creative hobby.

Remember, the key to sustainable self-care is aligning your routine with your specific needs and preferences. By understanding what areas require nurturing, you can tailor your self-care activities to meet those needs effectively. This assessment is the foundation upon which you'll build your personalized self-care routine. Once you've completed this step, we can move on to the next one.

2. Start Small:

Starting your self-care journey with small, manageable changes is crucial. Here's how to do it effectively:

- Avoid setting overly ambitious goals right from the start. If you aim too high too soon, you risk feeling overwhelmed, which can lead to frustration and abandonment of your routine.

- Instead, begin with tiny, achievable steps. For example, if your goal is to become more physically active, don't commit to a rigorous daily gym routine immediately. Instead, start with a 10-minute daily walk or a short workout session.

- These small changes may seem insignificant, but they serve a vital purpose: they help you build consistency and create a habit of self-care in your life.

By starting small, you'll be more likely to stick with your routine, and over time, you can gradually increase the complexity and duration of your self-care activities. This approach makes it easier to incorporate self-care into your daily life without feeling overwhelmed.

3. Make It a Habit:

Consistency is the key to turning self-care into a sustainable routine. Here's how to make it a habit:

- Set specific times during the day for your self-care activities. This helps establish a routine and makes it easier to integrate self-care into your daily life.
- Use reminders or alarms if necessary, especially when you're just starting. These prompts can help you remember to prioritize your self-care.
- Consider keeping a self-care journal. Document your activities, thoughts, and feelings related to self-care. This not only helps you track your progress but also reinforces the habit.

Creating a daily or weekly schedule for your self-care activities and sticking to it will help solidify these practices into your routine. Habits are formed through repetition, and making self-care a habit ensures that you consistently prioritize your well-being.

4. Be Flexible and Forgiving:

In your journey to establish a sustainable self-care routine, it's essential to remain adaptable and compassionate towards yourself. Here's how:

- Acknowledge that life can be unpredictable. There will be days when unexpected events or obligations disrupt your routine. This is entirely normal, and it's important not to be too hard on yourself during such times.

- Be forgiving and understanding when you miss a self-care activity or two. Self-care is about nurturing your well-being, not creating additional stress or guilt.

- Instead of dwelling on missed opportunities, focus on getting back on track as soon as you can. Remember that self-care is a lifelong practice, and occasional interruptions do not define your overall progress.

By maintaining flexibility and forgiveness, you ensure that your self-care routine remains sustainable and doesn't become a source of stress in itself. It's all about finding a balance that suits your lifestyle and needs.

5. Diversify Your Activities:

To keep your self-care routine engaging and effective, it's important to incorporate a variety of activities. Here's how to do it:

- If your focus is on physical health, don't limit yourself to a single exercise routine. Mix different types of exercises like cardio, strength training, and flexibility exercises to keep it interesting.

- For mental well-being, combine mindfulness practices such as meditation with intellectually stimulating activities like reading or learning a new skill.

- Explore hobbies and interests that bring you joy. These can include creative pursuits like painting, writing, or playing a musical instrument.

Diversity in your self-care activities not only prevents boredom but also ensures that you're addressing various aspects of your well-being. It helps keep your routine enjoyable and effective in nourishing your mind and body.

6. Regularly Re-evaluate:

As you progress with your self-care routine, it's essential to periodically assess its effectiveness and make adjustments when needed. Here's how to do this effectively:

- Take the time to reflect on your self-care routine regularly. What activities have been particularly beneficial, and which ones haven't made a significant impact?
- Consider any changes in your life, goals, or needs that may have occurred over time. Your self-care routine should evolve to accommodate these changes.
- Don't hesitate to make modifications and try new activities that align better with your current needs. Continuous adaptation keeps your self-care practice relevant and effective.

By regularly re-evaluating your self-care routine, you ensure that it remains tailored to your evolving needs, leading to better overall well-being.

7. Seek Community Support:

Incorporating a sense of community into your self-care journey can be highly beneficial. Here's how you can do that:

- Consider joining a group or community related to your self-care interests. Whether it's a fitness class, a book club, a meditation group, or any other community, being a part of such groups can provide motivation and support.

- Sharing your self-care journey with others can be a source of inspiration and accountability. Discussing your goals, progress, and challenges with like-minded individuals can help keep you on track.

- Collaborate with others in your community to explore new self-care activities or find creative ways to enhance your routine.

Having a supportive community around you can boost your commitment to self-care and make the journey more enjoyable. It's a valuable resource for encouragement and shared experiences.

8. Connect It to Your Long-Term Goals:

To give your self-care routine a deeper sense of purpose and direction, it's essential to align it with your long-term personal goals. Here's how you can do that:

- Identify your long-term goals and aspirations. These could be related to career, health, relationships, personal growth, or any area of your life that you want to improve.

- Ensure that your self-care routine includes activities that directly contribute to these goals. For example, if reducing stress is a long-term goal, incorporate stress-reduction activities like yoga, meditation, or journaling into your routine.

- Regularly reflect on how your self-care practices are helping you progress towards your long-term goals. This connection between self-care and your broader life objectives can provide motivation and a greater sense of purpose.

By aligning your self-care routine with your long-term goals, you ensure that your self-care practices are not just random acts but deliberate steps towards a more fulfilling and meaningful life. It creates a powerful synergy between self-care and personal growth.

Balancing Self-Care with Other Responsibilities

In the pursuit of a well-rounded life, balancing self-care with other responsibilities is crucial. This balance ensures that while you are taking care of your own needs, you are also effectively managing your other obligations - be it work, family, social, or personal commitments. Here's an in-depth guide on how to achieve this balance:

1. Prioritize Tasks and Responsibilities:

Balancing self-care with other responsibilities begins with understanding and prioritizing your various commitments. Here's how to go about it:

Understanding Priorities:

- Begin by identifying the key aspects of your life that hold the most importance for you. This could include your job, family, health, personal growth, or other specific commitments.
- Recognizing these priorities is crucial as it helps you allocate your limited time and energy more effectively.

Task Prioritization:

- Create a comprehensive list of your daily, weekly, and monthly tasks and responsibilities.

- Next, rank these tasks based on their urgency and importance. Urgent tasks require immediate attention, while important tasks may not be urgent but are equally vital.

- This practice of task prioritization enables you to focus on what needs immediate attention without neglecting less urgent but still important tasks.

By identifying and ranking your priorities, you'll have a clear roadmap for how to allocate your time and effort effectively. This foundational step sets the stage for achieving balance between self-care and your other responsibilities.

2. Integrate Self-Care into Your Daily Schedule:

Incorporating self-care into your daily routine is essential to ensure that it doesn't get neglected amidst your other responsibilities. Here's how you can do it:

Routine Integration:

- Instead of treating self-care as a separate activity, integrate it seamlessly into your daily schedule.

- For example, if you have a busy workday, consider incorporating short breaks for activities like deep breathing exercises or a brisk walk. These brief moments of self-care can rejuvenate you without taking up too much time.

Efficient Scheduling:

- Choose optimal times for your self-care activities when you're less likely to be interrupted or have other commitments.

- Early morning or late evening routines can be effective options since they often provide quieter, less hectic periods during the day.

By weaving self-care into your daily routine, it becomes a natural part of your day-to-day life, ensuring that you consistently prioritize your well-being alongside your other responsibilities.

3. Set Realistic Goals and Expectations:

Setting realistic goals and managing your expectations plays a crucial role in balancing self-care with your other responsibilities:

Realistic Goal Setting:

- When it comes to self-care, it's essential to set achievable goals. Recognize that you might have limitations in terms of time and resources.
- For instance, if you can only spare 15 minutes for exercise, it's more productive to focus on making the most of those 15 minutes rather than feeling pressured to do an hour-long workout.

Manage Expectations:

- Be realistic about what you can accomplish in a day. Overburdening yourself with an unrealistic to-do list can lead to stress and burnout, which are counterproductive to self-care.
- Understand that some days, your self-care routine may need to be shorter or adjusted due to unexpected responsibilities or commitments.

By setting achievable self-care goals and managing your daily expectations, you reduce the likelihood of feeling overwhelmed and increase your ability to maintain balance in your life.

4. Learn to Delegate and Ask for Help:

Balancing self-care becomes more manageable when you're willing to share responsibilities:

Delegating Tasks:

- You don't have to shoulder all tasks and responsibilities by yourself. At work and at home, identify tasks that can be delegated to others.
- Delegation can free up valuable time and energy that you can then allocate to self-care activities.

Seeking Support:

- Don't hesitate to ask for help when needed. Whether it's assistance with child care, household chores, or work assignments, reaching out for support can help you maintain your self-care routine.
- Seek support from colleagues, family members, or professionals where applicable.

By learning to delegate and seeking support, you create more room in your schedule for self-care without compromising your other responsibilities. This can significantly contribute to maintaining a balanced life.

5. Embrace the Art of Saying No:

Maintaining boundaries and learning when to say no is crucial in achieving a balance between self-care and other responsibilities:

Healthy Boundaries:

- Develop the ability to say no to requests or commitments that may interfere with your self-care or your top priorities.
- Setting boundaries is essential for safeguarding your time and energy.

Respect Your Limits:

- Acknowledge your limits and respect them. Understand that it's okay to decline additional responsibilities or commitments when your plate is already full.
- Saying no can be empowering and is an important part of self-care.

By embracing the art of saying no, you ensure that you don't overextend yourself and that you allocate your resources wisely to maintain a healthy balance in your life.

6. Utilize Time Management Techniques:

Efficiently managing your time is key to balancing self-care with other responsibilities:

Effective Planning:

- Utilize tools like planners, calendars, or productivity apps to organize your schedule.
- These tools help you visualize how your time is allocated and where you can fit in self-care activities.

Time Blocks:

- Consider using time-blocking methods where you designate specific blocks of time for different activities, including self-care.
- Allocating dedicated time slots for self-care ensures that you prioritize it alongside other commitments.

By implementing time management techniques, you can optimize your daily schedule, making it easier to integrate self-care without neglecting your other responsibilities.

7. Monitor and Adjust as Needed:

Balancing self-care with other responsibilities is an ongoing process that requires regular evaluation and adaptability:

Regular Check-ins:

- Periodically review your schedule and routines to assess how well you are maintaining the balance between self-care and your other obligations.
- Ask yourself questions like, "Are you managing to allocate time for self-care?" and "What adjustments can be made for better balance?"

Adaptability:

- Be open to adjusting your routine as circumstances change. Life is dynamic, and your responsibilities may shift over time.
- Flexibility is key to maintaining a balanced approach to self-care and other commitments.

By monitoring your progress and being adaptable, you ensure that you can make necessary adjustments to maintain a harmonious balance between self-care and your other responsibilities.

Balancing self-care with other responsibilities is about making conscious choices and adjustments to ensure that all aspects of your life receive the attention they deserve. It's about understanding that taking care of yourself is not a luxury, but a necessity that enables you to be more present, productive, and fulfilled in all areas of your life. Remember, a well-balanced life leads to improved overall well-being, happiness, and productivity.

BONUS Chapter: 9-Week Guided Self-Care Program

"Self-care is giving the world the best of you, instead of what's left of you." – (Reed)

Katie Reed is a mental health advocate and blogger known for her insightful commentary on parenting, mental health, and self-care. Through her writings and speeches, she has become a voice for acknowledging the challenges of mental health, especially in the context of motherhood and family life. Her work emphasizes the importance of self-care not only for personal well-being but also for being able to engage positively with others in one's life.

BONUS Chapter: 9-Week Guided Self-Care Program

Embark on a transformative expedition with the "Nine Week Guided Self-Care Program," a journey that's not just an escape but a deep dive into the essence of your well-being. Picture this program as your personal roadmap to rediscovery, where each step is a commitment to nurturing not only your physical health but also your emotional and spiritual vitality. This program is your invitation to a profound connection with yourself, crafted to reveal the layers of your inner world through the gentle art of self-care.

How to Use This Program:

1. **Weekly Focus:** Each week introduces a new dimension of self-care, starting with mindfulness and culminating in future-focused self-care planning. Dedicate yourself each week to fully immerse in the theme, allowing it to resonate with your daily experiences.

2. **Daily Practices:** The program thoughtfully outlines specific activities or practices assigned for five days each week, each thoughtfully designed to build upon the previous one. These daily steps, spread across the week, will weave together into a comprehensive tapestry of self-care routines by the program's end. Notably, two days per week are left intentionally free from assigned practices, allowing time for reflection, rest, or personal discretion in self-care activities.

3. **Set a Regular Time:** Establish a routine by performing your self-care activities at the same time daily. Whether it's a quiet morning meditation or an evening gratitude session, a consistent schedule helps these practices evolve into enduring habits.

4. **Create Your Space:** Designate a special area in your home for your self-care activities. This could be a tranquil corner for meditation or a cozy nook for

journaling. This physical space serves as a sanctuary for your self-care journey.

Getting the Most Out of the Program:

1. **Reflect and Journal:** Maintain a journal throughout the program. Post-practice reflections and journaling deepen the experience and provide a valuable record of your journey.

2. **Embrace Each Step:** Keep an open mind toward each week's focus. Even if a practice feels unfamiliar, engaging with it can open doors to unexpected personal insights.

3. **Stay Connected:** Share your journey with others participating in the program. The shared experiences and support can significantly enrich your journey.

4. **Adapt as Needed:** Personalize the practices to suit your unique needs. Modify or substitute exercises to align more closely with your personal journey.

5. **Practice Patience and Kindness:** Throughout this process, treat yourself with patience and kindness, especially on more challenging days. Remember that self-care is about the journey, not just the destination.

6. **Celebrate Small Wins:** Recognize and celebrate your progress. Each step, no matter its size, is a milestone in enhancing your well-being.

The "Nine Week Guided Self-Care Program" invites you to embark on a transformative journey of growth and self-discovery. By actively engaging with each week's theme and daily practices, this program will incorporate all the aspects of self-care you have learned so far, allowing you to gradually cultivate a rich and sustainable self-care routine. It goes beyond being a mere series of activities; instead, it's a profound journey toward establishing a lifelong practice of mindfulness, self-compassion, and proactive well-being.

Week 1: Introduction to Mindfulness:

Welcome to Week 1 of our "Mindful Living" journey. This week, we'll lay the foundation for a mindful and balanced life. Mindfulness is the practice of being fully present in the moment, and it's an essential skill for self-care.

Day 1 - Mindful Breathing:

Mindful breathing is a foundational practice in mindfulness, a technique that can bring tranquility and heightened awareness to your daily life. To embark on this journey, follow this comprehensive guide:

- **Choose a Quiet Space:** To begin your mindful breathing practice, it's essential to find a quiet and comfortable space where you won't be disturbed. This environment will help you fully immerse yourself in the experience.

- **Comfortable Seating:** Once you've found your serene space, select a chair or cushion that supports a relaxed yet upright posture. Your back should remain straight but not stiff, allowing for a natural flow of breath. Rest your hands gently on your lap, fostering a sense of relaxation and ease.

- **Focus on Your Breath:** With your posture settled, close your eyes if you feel comfortable doing so. Begin the practice by taking a few initial breaths. These initial breaths serve as a transition into a more mindful state.

- **Inhale Slowly:** As you continue, direct your attention to your breath. Inhale deeply through your nose, counting to four as you do so. With each inhalation, let the breath fill your lungs completely, expanding your chest and abdomen. Notice the sensation of the breath as it enters your nostrils and flows inward.

- **Exhale Gradually:** Following your deep inhalation, exhale slowly and deliberately through your mouth. Maintain the count of four as you release the breath. As you exhale, focus on the sensation of releasing any tension or stress that may be held within your body. Let it flow out with each breath.

- **Repeat and Maintain Focus:** Continue this mindful breathing exercise for a few minutes or even longer, depending on your preference and available time. The key is to sustain your attention on your breath. If your mind begins to wander, which is a natural occurrence, gently guide your focus back to your breath. Be patient with yourself; the practice is about returning to the present moment with kindness.

Mindful breathing serves as a foundational building block for mindfulness, helping you ground yourself in the present and fostering a deep sense of relaxation. Regular practice can lead to reduced stress, improved focus, and an enhanced overall sense of well-being. As you continue this journey, you'll find that your ability to stay present and cultivate inner peace grows stronger with each session.

Day 2 - Mindful Eating:

Mindful eating is a practice that goes beyond simply nourishing your body; it encourages a profound appreciation for your food and a deeper connection with what you consume. Here's a guide:

- **Set the Scene:** Choose a quiet, pleasant place to eat without distractions like phones or TV. Selecting the right environment is crucial for mindful eating. Find a space that promotes relaxation and enjoyment of your meal. It could be your dining room, a peaceful garden, or a cozy corner with soft lighting. Turn off electronic devices and put them away.

- **Engage Your Senses:** As you sit down to eat, observe the colors, shapes, and arrangement of the food on your plate. As you take your first bite, explore the various flavors that unfold. Identify the sweetness, saltiness, spiciness, and textures in each mouthful. Let your taste buds revel in the rich tapestry of tastes and sensations. To fully appreciate the flavors and textures, chew slowly and deliberately. Feel the food breaking down in your mouth. This not only enhances the eating experience but also aids in digestion.

- **Mindful Bites:** Instead of rushing through your meal, savor each bite as if it were the most delicious thing you've ever tasted. Be present with every mouthful, appreciating the intricate flavors and textures. After each bite, gently place your utensil down and pause. This simple act encourages mindfulness and prevents mindless eating. It allows you to assess your level of fullness before taking the next bite.

- **Observe Your Body:** Pay attention to your body's signals of hunger and fullness during your meal. Are you genuinely hungry, or are you eating out of habit, boredom, or emotions? Mindful eating helps you distinguish between physical and emotional hunger. Eat until you feel satisfied, not until you're overly full. Tuning in to your body's cues allows you to avoid overeating, which can lead to discomfort and unwanted consequences.

- **Gratitude:** As you enjoy your meal, take a moment to reflect on the journey your food has taken before reaching your plate. Consider the farmers who grew the ingredients, the hands that harvested them, and the cooks who prepared the meal. Express gratitude for the nourishment and sustenance your meal provides. Recognize that not everyone has access to such food, and be thankful for what you have.

Mindful eating is a practice that can transform the way you relate to food, fostering a deeper connection and appreciation for each meal. It encourages healthier eating habits, reduces overeating, and promotes a sense of fulfillment beyond just physical nourishment. As you continue to incorporate mindfulness into your meals, you'll discover a richer and more gratifying relationship with food and nourishment.

Day 3 - Mindful Walking:

Mindful walking is a practice that invites you to connect with nature or any serene environment in a profound way. Here's how you can immerse yourself in this experience:

Begin by selecting a natural setting that resonates with you, whether it's a tranquil park, a serene beach, a forest, or simply a quiet neighborhood street. The choice of location should be free from distractions and allow you to walk comfortably and safely.

As you start your mindful walk, focus on these aspects:

- **Feel the Ground Beneath Your Feet:** Pay attention to each step you take. Feel the texture of the ground beneath your feet. Notice the variations in terrain, whether it's the softness of grass, the solidity of pavement, or the coolness of sand. Sensations of touch ground you in the present moment.

- **Listen to the Sounds Around You:** Tune in to the soundscape of your surroundings. Listen to the chirping of birds, the rustling of leaves, the gentle flow of water, or the distant hum of city life. These auditory experiences anchor you in the present, and there's no need to judge or analyze the sounds; simply observe them.

- **Observe the World Without Judgment:** As you walk, open your awareness to the world around you. Observe the colors, shapes, and patterns in nature.

Be mindful of the flora and fauna you encounter without forming judgments or labels. Let go of the need to categorize or evaluate what you see.

- **Breathe Mindfully:** Don't forget to bring your mindful breathing into your walking practice. Pay attention to your breath as it synchronizes with your steps. Inhale slowly through your nose and exhale through your mouth, allowing each breath to center you further.

- **Connect with Your Body:** Pay attention to the physical sensations within your body as you walk. Notice the gentle rhythm of your breathing, the feeling of your muscles moving, and the way your feet make contact with the ground. Feel the connection between your body and the Earth beneath you.

- **Practice Gratitude:** As you continue your mindful walk, take moments to express gratitude for the natural world around you. Be thankful for the opportunity to connect with the environment and for the beauty it offers.

By mindfully walking, you're not only connecting with nature but also cultivating a deep sense of presence and peace. This practice encourages you to let go of the past and future, embracing the beauty of the here and now. It's an opportunity to experience the world with fresh eyes, free from judgment or preconceived notions. As you continue to engage in mindful walking, you may find it to be a restorative and grounding activity that enhances your overall well-being.

Day 4 - Mindful Daily Routine:

Mindfulness practice isn't limited to specific meditation sessions or quiet moments of reflection. It extends into your daily life, transforming routine activities into opportunities for presence and awareness. Here's how you can apply mindfulness to your daily activities:

- **Choose Your Activity:** Begin by selecting a routine task to focus on. This could be anything from washing dishes, taking a shower, making your bed, or even your morning cup of tea.

- **Set the Intention:** Before you commence the activity, set the intention to be fully present in each action. Understand that this task, no matter how mundane, has the potential to be a mindful experience.

- **Engage All Your Senses:** As you start the task, engage all your senses. Feel the sensations of the activity. Whether it's the warm water on your hands while washing dishes, the texture of your towel after a shower, or the sensation of brushing your teeth, immerse yourself in the physicality of the moment. Pay attention to the visual aspects. Observe the details around you—the soap bubbles in the sink, the patterns of tiles in the shower, or the bristles of your toothbrush. Be present with what you see. Notice any scents or aromas associated with the task. Whether it's the aroma of soap, the freshness of your shampoo, or the toothpaste, inhale deeply and appreciate the smells. Listen actively to the sounds of the activity. Hear the running water, the rustling of clothes, or the brushing of your teeth. These sounds are part of the experience.

- **Stay Fully Present:** As you continue with the task, anchor your focus on what you're doing. Resist the urge to let your mind wander to past or future concerns. If your thoughts do drift, gently guide them back to the task at hand.

- **Mindful Movements:** Pay attention to the movements involved in the activity. Whether it's the rhythm of scrubbing dishes, the way you wash your hair or the precise motion of brushing your teeth, be fully present in each action.

- **Breathe Mindfully:** Just as in other mindfulness practices, don't forget to bring your attention to your breath. Breathe deeply and steadily as you engage in your task. Your breath can serve as an anchor, bringing you back to the present moment.

- **Gratitude and Presence:** Conclude the task with a moment of gratitude. Recognize that even the most routine activities are moments of life that you've experienced fully. Be grateful for the simple, everyday experiences that make up your life.

Applying mindfulness to your daily routine can infuse a sense of purpose and awareness into seemingly ordinary tasks. It allows you to break free from autopilot mode and truly experience each moment as it unfolds. Over time, this practice can lead to reduced stress, increased focus, and a deeper sense of fulfillment in your daily life. Remember, mindfulness isn't about changing what you do; it's about changing how you do it, with presence and intention.

Day 5 - Reflection:

Reflection is a crucial part of mindfulness practice, as it allows you to process your experiences and gain deeper insights into your journey. Take time to journal about your experiences from the past week, noting any changes in your awareness or sense of calm. Here's a comprehensive guide:

- **Prepare Your Journal:** Begin by setting up your journal or a dedicated notebook for this reflection. Find a quiet and comfortable space where you can focus without interruptions.

- **Review Your Mindful Practices:** Take a moment to recall the mindful activities you've engaged in throughout the week. This could include mindful breathing, eating, walking, and integrating mindfulness into your daily routine. Reflect on your commitment to these practices.

- **Changes in Awareness:** Explore any shifts in your awareness that you've noticed during the week. Have you become more attuned to the present moment? Are you more conscious of your thoughts and emotions? Have you observed any changes in how you perceive your surroundings or interact with others?

- **Sense of Calm:** Reflect on your sense of calm. Has it evolved over the past week? Do you find it easier to remain composed in challenging situations? Notice any moments of inner peace or tranquility that you've experienced.

- **Challenges and Observations:** Be honest with yourself about any challenges you encountered during your mindfulness journey. Did you find it difficult to stay present at times? Were there moments of distraction or restlessness? Use these observations as opportunities for growth and learning.

- **Gratitude:** Express gratitude for the progress you've made, no matter how small it may seem. Recognize that mindfulness is a practice, and each step forward is a valuable achievement. Be thankful for your dedication to self-improvement.

- **Set Intentions:** Consider what you'd like to focus on in the upcoming week. Are there specific aspects of mindfulness you'd like to deepen? Do you have any goals or intentions for your practice moving forward? Setting clear intentions can guide your mindfulness journey.

- **Self-Compassion:** Throughout your reflection, practice self-compassion. Embrace any imperfections or challenges with kindness and understanding. Mindfulness is a journey of self-discovery, and it's natural to have ups and downs along the way.

- **Regular Practice:** Make reflection a regular part of your mindfulness practice. It helps you track your progress, identify areas for improvement, and maintain motivation.

Journaling about your mindfulness experiences enhances your self-awareness and reinforces the positive changes mindfulness can bring to your life. It's a powerful tool for self-reflection and personal growth. As you continue your mindfulness journey, remember that it's an ongoing process, and each reflection deepens your connection with yourself and the world around you.

Congratulations on completing your first week of the Introduction to Mindfulness journey! This week has been a foundational step toward greater self-awareness and enhanced well-being through mindfulness practices.

As you move forward, remember that mindfulness is a journey, not a destination. Each day of practice brings you closer to a more mindful and fulfilling life. Embrace the journey with patience and kindness toward yourself. Stay tuned for Week 2, where you'll explore advanced mindfulness techniques to further enrich your mindfulness practice and well-being.

Week 2: Deepening Mindfulness Practice:

Welcome to Week 2 of our "Mindful Living" journey. Now that you've laid the groundwork with basic mindfulness practices, we'll delve deeper into the art of being present and fully engaged with your experiences.

Day 1 - Body Scan Meditation:

Body scan meditation is a powerful mindfulness practice that enhances your awareness of physical sensations and promotes relaxation. Here's a step-by-step guide for a deep and immersive experience:

- **Find a Comfortable Space**: Begin by locating a quiet and comfortable space where you can lie down without distractions. It's best to use a yoga mat, blanket, or soft surface to support your body.

- **Lie Down and Close Your Eyes:** Lie down on your back with your legs slightly apart and your arms resting at your sides. Close your eyes gently. This position allows your body to relax fully.

- **Focus on Your Breath:** Start by taking a few deep breaths to settle into the meditation. Inhale slowly through your nose, allowing your abdomen to rise as you fill your lungs. Exhale gently through your mouth, releasing any tension.

- **Begin the Scan:** Now, mentally scan your body from head to toe. Imagine a warm, soft light starting at the crown of your head and slowly moving down through your body. As this imaginary light passes through each part of your body, focus your attention on that area.

- **Release Tension:** If you notice any tension or discomfort during the scan, consciously release it. Imagine the tension melting away like ice melting in warm water. Use your breath to help you let go of any tightness.

- **Move Slowly:** Progress through the body scan at a deliberate, unhurried pace. Take your time with each area, allowing yourself to fully explore the sensations present.

- **Complete the Scan:** Once you've reached your toes, take a moment to appreciate your entire body as a whole. Feel the sense of relaxation and awareness that has emerged during this practice.

- **Breathe Mindfully:** Conclude the body scan by returning your focus to your breath. Take a few more mindful breaths, inhaling and exhaling slowly, enjoying the sense of calm that this meditation has cultivated.

- **Open Your Eyes:** When you're ready, open your eyes gently, taking a moment to reacquaint yourself with your surroundings.

Body scan meditation is an excellent way to develop a profound connection with your body, release tension, and enhance self-awareness. It can be especially beneficial for managing stress and promoting relaxation. As you practice this meditation regularly, you'll find that your ability to stay present and attuned to your physical sensations improves, enriching your overall mindfulness journey.

Day 2 - Mindful Observation:

Mindful observation is a practice that deepens your awareness of the world around you, allowing you to find beauty and meaning in everyday objects. Here's a comprehensive guide:

- **Select an Object:** Begin by selecting an object in your immediate surroundings. It could be a flower, a piece of art, a household item like a cup, or anything that catches your eye.

- **Find a Quiet Space:** Choose a quiet and comfortable space where you can sit or stand with the selected object in front of you. Ensure there are minimal distractions.

- **Focus Your Gaze:** Direct your attention to the chosen object. Allow your gaze to settle on it, and make a commitment to explore it with fresh eyes, as if you're seeing it for the first time.

- **Observe Details:** Start to observe the object closely, paying attention to every detail. Notice its shape, color, texture, and any patterns or imperfections. Let your eyes linger on each feature.

- **Engage Your Senses:** As you observe, engage your senses fully. If it's an object you can touch, gently run your fingers over it, feeling its surface. If it's an item with a scent, take a moment to inhale and appreciate its aroma. Immerse yourself in the sensory experience.

- **Shift Perspective:** Try to look at the object from different angles or perspectives. See how the lighting affects its appearance. Observe how your perception of the object changes as you shift your viewpoint.

- **Mindful Breathing:** As you continue to observe, use your breath as an anchor to stay present. Take slow, deep breaths, inhaling through your nose and exhaling through your mouth. Your breath helps you maintain focus and calm.

- **Let Go of Labels:** During this practice, avoid labeling or judging the object. Instead, cultivate a sense of wonder and curiosity. Approach it with the openness of a beginner's mind.

- **Observe Emotions:** Pay attention to any emotions or thoughts that arise during this observation. You might feel a sense of appreciation, curiosity, or even surprise. Acknowledge these feelings without attachment.

- **Reflect:** After you've spent ample time observing the object, take a moment to reflect on the experience. Consider how this practice of mindful observation has allowed you to perceive the beauty and complexity in something you might usually overlook.

Mindful observation opens your eyes to the richness of the present moment and encourages a deeper connection with the world around you. It fosters a sense of gratitude and appreciation for the ordinary, transforming the mundane into something extraordinary. As you practice this regularly, you'll find that mindful observation enriches your mindfulness journey and helps you find beauty and meaning in even the simplest aspects of life.

Day 3 - Mindful Listening:

Mindful listening is a practice that cultivates deep awareness of the sounds in your environment, allowing you to connect with the present moment through your sense of hearing. Here's a comprehensive guide:

- **Choose a Quiet Setting**: Begin by selecting a quiet and peaceful setting where you can sit comfortably. This could be indoors or outdoors, as long as it's free from distracting noises.

- **Assume a Comfortable Posture:** Sit down in a relaxed but attentive posture. You can sit on a chair or cushion with your back straight and your hands resting on your lap. Close your eyes gently to eliminate visual distractions, if you're comfortable doing so.

- **Begin with Breath Awareness:** Start by taking a few deep and mindful breaths to settle into the practice. Inhale slowly through your nose, allowing your abdomen to expand, and exhale gently through your mouth. This helps you anchor your focus on the present moment.

- **Open Your Ears:** Shift your attention to the sounds around you. Listen actively and without judgment. Allow the sounds to enter your awareness without labeling them or forming opinions about them.

- **Expand Your Listening:** Gradually expand your listening awareness to include both near and distant sounds. Pay attention to subtle sounds that you might typically overlook, such as the rustling of leaves, distant traffic, or the chirping of birds.

- **Notice Layers of Sound:** Observe the different layers of sound in your environment. Recognize that various sounds coexist simultaneously. Let go of any urge to analyze or identify specific sounds; simply be present with the auditory experience.

- **Use Your Breath as an Anchor:** If your mind starts to wander or you become distracted by thoughts, gently bring your focus back to your breath. Use each breath as an anchor to stay rooted in the practice of mindful listening.

- **Deepen Your Listening:** As you continue to listen mindfully, notice how your perception of sound deepens. You may become more attuned to subtleties, such as variations in pitch, rhythm, and volume.

- **Reflect on the Practice:** After a sufficient period of mindful listening, gradually shift your awareness back to your breath. Take a moment to reflect on the practice. Consider how this exercise has allowed you to connect with the world through your sense of hearing and appreciate the richness of the present moment.

Mindful listening is a practice that tunes you into the symphony of sounds that surround you, promoting a sense of presence and deepening your connection with the world. As you incorporate this practice into your routine, you'll find that it heightens your awareness, fosters a sense of tranquility, and enhances your overall self-care journey.

Day 4 - Mindful Movement:

Mindful movement invites you to integrate mindfulness into physical activities, allowing you to be fully present in your body and breath during movement. Here's a comprehensive guide:

- **Select Your Activity:** Begin by choosing a physical activity for the day. It could be yoga, stretching, a short walk, or any form of movement that you enjoy. The key is to select an activity that allows you to connect with your body and breath.

- **Find a Suitable Space:** Locate a quiet and safe space where you can engage in your chosen movement practice. Ensure you have enough room to move comfortably.

- **Set an Intention:** Before you start, set an intention for your mindful movement practice. Consider what you'd like to focus on or experience during the activity. It could be relaxation, increased flexibility, or simply being fully present.

- **Begin with Breath Awareness:** Start your movement practice by focusing on your breath. Take a few deep, intentional breaths to center yourself. Inhale through your nose, and exhale through your mouth.

- **Connect with Your Body:** As you move, pay close attention to the sensations in your body. Notice how your muscles engage, how your joints move, and the rhythm of your breath. Be fully present with each movement.

- **Move Deliberately:** Perform each movement slowly and deliberately. Avoid rushing or moving mechanically. Whether it's a yoga pose, a stretch, or a simple walk, focus on the quality of each movement rather than quantity.

- **Stay Present:** If your mind starts to wander or become distracted, gently redirect your focus to the sensations in your body and your breath. Mindful movement is about being in the moment.

- **Breath and Movement Synchronization:** Pay attention to the coordination of your breath with your movements. Inhale as you expand or lengthen, and exhale as you contract or release. This synchronization deepens your mindfulness.

- **Observe Your Thoughts:** Be aware of any thoughts or judgments that arise during your mindful movement practice. Allow them to come and go without attachment. Your focus remains on the physical experience.

- **Conclude Mindfully:** As you conclude your movement practice, take a moment to stand or sit quietly. Reflect on how the practice made you feel both physically and mentally. Express gratitude for the opportunity to connect with your body in this way.

Mindful movement allows you to infuse everyday physical activities with mindfulness, promoting a sense of presence and inner calm. Regularly incorporating this practice into your routine enhances your body-mind connection and enriches your overall life.

Day 5 - Reflect and Share:

Reflecting on your sel-care practices and sharing your experiences can deepen your understanding and create a sense of community. Here's a comprehensive guide:

- **Prepare Your Space:** Find a quiet and comfortable space where you can sit down with your journal or a notebook. Ensure you have some dedicated time for reflection.

- **Retrieve Your Journal:** If you've been journaling throughout the week, retrieve your journal. It's where you've documented your experiences and insights from the previous days.

- **Review Your Practices:** Begin by reviewing the mindfulness practices you've engaged in throughout the week. This includes mindful body scanning, observation, listening, and movement. Take note of any shifts in your awareness or feelings of calm you've experienced.

- **Reflect on Insights:** Reflect on any insights or observations that have emerged during your mindfulness journey this week. These could be personal realizations, changes in your perception, or moments of increased awareness.

- **Express Your Feelings:** Use your journal as a space to express your feelings and emotions. Share any challenges you've encountered and how you navigated them. Celebrate your successes and acknowledge areas for growth.

- **Share with Others:** If you're part of a mindfulness program or an online community, consider sharing your experiences with others. Engaging in open and honest discussions with fellow practitioners can provide support and inspire further insights.

- **Express Gratitude**: Take a moment to express gratitude for the opportunity to explore mindfulness and deepen your self-awareness. Recognize the effort and dedication you've put into this practice.

- **Set Intentions:** As you conclude your reflection, consider setting intentions for the upcoming week. What aspects of mindfulness would you like to focus on? Are there specific goals or practices you'd like to incorporate into your routine?

- **Share with Loved Ones:** If you're comfortable, share your mindfulness experiences with friends or family members. Sharing your journey can inspire others and create meaningful connections.

- **Commit to Continuation:** Finally, reaffirm your commitment to your mindfulness journey. Recognize that mindfulness is an ongoing practice, and each reflection and sharing session deepens your connection with yourself and the world.

Reflecting and sharing are integral components of mindfulness practice. They allow you to process your experiences, gain insights, and connect with others who are on a similar journey. As you continue your inner exploration, remember that self-awareness is a profound gift, and sharing it with others can enrich both your personal growth and the sense of community within your self-care program or circle.

Deepening Mindfulness Practice – Week 2 Review:

During Week 2, you've taken significant steps in deepening your mindfulness practice. You've explored various techniques that have allowed you to connect more profoundly with the present moment and your inner self.

As you progress, remember that deepening your mindfulness practice is an ongoing journey of self-discovery. Each day brings new insights and a stronger connection to the present moment. Stay tuned for Week 3, where you'll explore Emotional Wellness and Self-Discovery, continuing your path towards greater self-awareness and overall well-being.

Week 3: Emotional Wellness and Self-Discovery:

Welcome to Week 3 of our "Mindful Living" journey. This week, we'll delve into the realm of emotions, gratitude, and the power of journaling as tools for emotional well-being.

Day 1 - Emotion Identification:

Emotion identification is a fundamental practice in emotional wellness and self-discovery. It involves acknowledging and labeling your emotions throughout the day.

- **Morning Awareness:** Start your day by setting an intention to pay close attention to your emotions. As you wake up, take a few moments to check in with yourself. Notice how you're feeling emotionally, physically, and mentally.

- **Emotion Naming:** Throughout the day, pause at various intervals to identify and name your emotions. This practice encourages self-awareness and emotional intelligence. When you experience an emotion, pause and say to yourself, "I am feeling [emotion]." Be specific in your emotional identification. For example, you might identify feelings such as joy, frustration, contentment, or anxiety.

- **Use a Journal:** Consider keeping a small journal or notepad with you during the day. Whenever you identify an emotion, jot it down along with a brief note about the situation or context in which it arose. This can help you track patterns in your emotional responses.

- **Practice Non-Judgment:** As you name your emotions, practice non-judgment. Avoid labeling your emotions as "good" or "bad." Instead, view them as valuable sources of information about your inner state.

- **Reflect on Triggers:** When you identify an emotion, reflect on what triggered it. Was it a specific event, interaction, or thought? Understanding the triggers can provide insight into the roots of your emotions.

- **Acceptance and Compassion:** If you notice challenging emotions, such as anger or sadness, approach them with self-compassion. Recognize that it's okay to feel these emotions, and they don't define your worth.

- **Evening Reflection:** At the end of the day, take some time to review your emotional notes. Reflect on any patterns or recurring emotions you've identified. This reflection can deepen your understanding of your emotional landscape.

- **Set an Intention:** Before you go to sleep, set an intention for the next day. Consider how you'd like to approach your emotions with awareness and acceptance. Emphasize the importance of emotional well-being in your journey.

Emotion identification is a practice that enhances self-awareness, emotional intelligence, and overall emotional well-being. As you continue this practice, you'll become more attuned to your inner world, gaining valuable insights into your emotional responses and fostering a deeper connection with yourself.

Day 2 - Gratitude Practice:

Gratitude practice is a powerful way to cultivate positive emotions and enhance your emotional well-being. Here's a guide for todays' practice:

- **Morning Reflection:** Begin your day with a few moments of quiet reflection. Find a comfortable and peaceful space where you can sit or even lie down. Take a few deep breaths to center yourself.

- **Create Your Gratitude List:** In your journal, start creating a list of things you're thankful for. Reflect on both big and small blessings in your life. These could be relationships, experiences, material possessions, or even moments of serenity.

- **Specificity is Key:** When listing your blessings, be specific. Instead of just saying you're grateful for family, specify what about your family brings you joy or support. The more specific you are, the deeper your sense of gratitude becomes.

- **Mindful Reflection:** As you write down each item, take a moment to truly reflect on it. Visualize the people, experiences, or things you're grateful for. Allow yourself to feel the positive emotions associated with them.

- **Daily Ritual:** Consider making this gratitude practice a daily ritual. Each morning or evening, add new items to your gratitude list. Over time, you'll accumulate a wealth of positive moments and blessings.

- **Express Thanks:** If you can, express your gratitude to those who have played a role in your blessings. Whether it's a simple thank-you note, a heartfelt conversation, or a kind gesture, expressing your thanks can deepen your sense of gratitude.

- **Pause Throughout the Day:** Beyond your journaling session, pause at various points during the day to mentally acknowledge things you're grateful for. This practice can infuse your day with positivity.

- **Evening Reflection:** Before you go to bed, revisit your gratitude list. Take a few moments to read through it and savor the feelings of gratitude to end your day on a positive note.

- **Variety Matters:** Challenge yourself to find new things to be grateful for each day. This encourages you to actively seek out the positive aspects of life.

- **Gratitude as a Mindset**: Over time, cultivate gratitude as a mindset. Instead of merely listing things you're grateful for, try to view the world with an underlying attitude of gratitude. This can transform how you perceive and respond to daily experiences.

Gratitude practice is a powerful tool for enhancing emotional well-being. It shifts your focus from what might be lacking in your life to what you already have and cherish. By consistently nurturing gratitude, you'll find that positive emotions become more prominent, and you develop a deeper sense of contentment and fulfillment.

Day 3 - Journaling for Emotional Awareness:

Journaling for emotional awareness is a transformative practice that allows you to explore and process your feelings honestly and non-judgmentally.

- **Select Your Journal:** Begin by choosing a dedicated journal or notebook for your emotional awareness practice. This journal will be a safe space for you to express your thoughts and feelings.

- **Create a Calm Environment:** Find a quiet and comfortable place where you can sit down with your journal. Ensure you won't be disturbed during your journaling session.

- **Start with Reflection:** Begin your journaling session by taking a few moments to reflect on your current emotional state. How are you feeling in this moment? What emotions are present? Note any physical sensations associated with these emotions.

- **Write Freely:** Write freely and without self-censorship. Allow your thoughts and emotions to flow onto the pages. Don't worry about grammar or structure; this practice is for your personal exploration.

- **Identify Emotions:** Be specific about the emotions you're experiencing. Use descriptive words to capture the nuances of your feelings. For example, instead of just writing "I feel sad," you might elaborate on why you feel sad and what it feels like.

- **Explore Triggers**: Reflect on the events or situations that may have triggered your emotions. Dive deeper into the underlying causes and explore any patterns or recurring themes in your emotional responses.

- **Express Without Judgment:** Practice non-judgment and self-compassion as you write. Avoid labeling your emotions as right or wrong, accept them as valid responses to your experiences.

- **Ask Open-Ended Questions:** Consider asking open-ended questions in your journal to prompt deeper reflection. For instance, "What can I learn from this emotion?" or "How can I respond to this feeling in a healthy way?"

- **Embrace Uncertainty:** If you encounter uncertainty or confusion about your emotions, embrace it. It's okay not to have all the answers. Journaling can help you explore and navigate these uncertainties.

- **Conclude with Gratitude:** As you conclude your journaling session, write down a few things you're grateful for, which can help balance your emotional exploration with positivity.

- **Regular Practice:** Make journaling for emotional awareness a regular practice. Set aside time each day or as needed to engage in this reflective exercise.

Journaling for emotional awareness is a profound tool for understanding your inner world, processing emotions, and gaining clarity about your emotional responses. As you continue this practice, you'll become more attuned to your feelings, allowing you to navigate them with greater insight and emotional intelligence.

Day 4 - Creative Expression:

Creative expression empowers you to process and convey your emotions through art. It allows you to choose from a range of artistic mediums to explore and communicate your feelings. Follow these steps to engage in this practice:

- **Select Your Medium:** Begin by picking a creative medium that resonates with you. Whether it's painting, drawing, writing poetry, composing music, dancing, or any other form of artistic expression, choose what aligns with your creativity.

- **Create a Supportive Environment:** Find a comfortable, distraction-free space where you can immerse yourself in your chosen creative outlet. Set up your art supplies or prepare your creative area accordingly.

- **Embrace Emotional Exploration:** Before you start, take a moment to connect with your emotions. Reflect on the feelings you intend to convey or explore through your creative endeavor. Consider how colors, shapes, or movements can represent these emotions.

- **Begin Crafting:** Dive into the creative process without self-criticism. Use your chosen medium as a channel to express your emotions. Allow colors, strokes, words, or movements to authentically mirror your feelings.

- **Non-Verbal Expression:** Keep in mind that creative expression transcends words. Let your chosen medium convey your emotions through symbols, hues, gestures, or non-verbal communication.

- **Practice Mindful Presence:** Stay fully engaged in the creative process. Pay attention to the sensations and emotions that emerge as you work. Allow your intuition to guide your creation.

- **Embrace Imperfection:** Remember that creative expression isn't about achieving perfection. It's about genuine self-expression. Embrace imperfections and release the need for flawlessness.

- **Reflect on Your Artwork:** After completing your creative piece, take time to reflect on it. Explore the emotions it evokes in you and the way it reflects your inner world. Delve into the symbolism and meaning behind your creation.

- **Share if Comfortable:** If you feel at ease, share your artistic expression with a trusted person. Alternatively, keep it private if you prefer. Sharing can foster connections with others and offer fresh insights into your emotions.

- **Repeat as Needed:** Creative expression is an ongoing practice. Whenever the urge arises to explore or communicate your emotions through art, return to this practice.

Creative expression empowers you to give your emotions a tangible form and delve into their depths. It provides an outlet for self-expression and offers a therapeutic means to process and understand your feelings. As you continue exploring different creative mediums, you'll notice that your emotional awareness and artistic skills flourish hand in hand.

Day 5 - Sharing Feelings:

Sharing your emotional experiences with someone you trust is a significant step in emotional wellness and self-discovery.

- **Select Your Trusted Listener:** Choose a person you trust and feel comfortable with to share your feelings. This could be a close friend, family member, partner, or even a therapist. Ensure that the individual is supportive and empathetic.

- **Set the Right Environment:** Find a quiet and comfortable setting where you can have an open and honest conversation. Minimize distractions and create a safe space for sharing.

- **Prepare Yourself:** Before you begin, take a moment to collect your thoughts and emotions. Reflect on what you'd like to share and why it's essential to you.

- **Express Your Emotions:** When you start the conversation, begin by expressing your emotions honestly and openly. Use "I" statements to describe how you feel. For example, say, "I've been feeling overwhelmed lately," rather than, "You make me feel overwhelmed."

- **Share Your Experiences:** Share specific experiences or situations that have triggered your emotions. Offer context and background to help the listener understand your perspective.

- **Be Vulnerable:** Allow yourself to be vulnerable during the conversation. It's okay to show your emotions and express vulnerability. This can deepen the connection and understanding between you and your listener.

- **Active Listening:** Encourage your listener to actively listen without judgment. Ask them to refrain from offering solutions or advice unless you explicitly request it.

- **Ask for Support:** If you require specific support or assistance, don't hesitate to ask for it. Whether it's emotional support, advice, or simply someone to listen, make your needs clear.

- **Empathize and Validate:** As you share, listen to the responses and feedback from your trusted listener. They may offer empathy, validation, or similar experiences of their own.

- **Reflect and Process:** After the conversation, take some time to reflect on how sharing your feelings impacted you. Consider whether it provided relief, clarity, or deeper understanding.

- **Express Gratitude:** Regardless of the outcome, express gratitude to your listener for being there for you and offering their support. A simple "thank you" can go a long way in maintaining strong relationships.

- **Offer Reciprocity:** Remember that sharing feelings is a two-way street. Be open to listening and supporting your trusted listener when they need it. Mutual emotional support strengthens relationships.

Sharing your feelings with a trusted person is an essential aspect of emotional wellness. It allows you to release pent-up emotions, gain fresh perspectives, and deepen your connections with others. This practice promotes self-discovery and reminds you that you're not alone on your emotional journey.

During the past week, you delved into the realm of "Emotional Wellness and Self-Discovery." This transformative journey allowed you to explore and navigate the intricate landscape of your emotions, fostering a deeper understanding of yourself.

As you reflect on the past week, you can acknowledge the growth and self-discovery that unfolded. You nurtured emotional well-being by embracing your feelings and actively exploring their depths. Remember that self-discovery is a vital step toward holistic well-being, and each day brought you closer to a more profound understanding of yourself.

Stay tuned for Week 4, where the focus will shift to "Developing Emotional Intelligence." This journey promises further insights and tools to enhance your emotional well-being and self-awareness.

Week 4: Developing Emotional Intelligence:

Welcome to Week 4 of our "Mindful Living" journey. This week, we'll delve into emotional intelligence, which is the ability to understand and manage your emotions effectively. These skills are vital for enhancing your overall emotional well-being.

Day 1 – Understanding Emotions:

Day 1 focuses on deepening your understanding of emotions, a fundamental step in developing emotional intelligence. This practice will help you explore various aspects of emotions and their impact on your daily life. Here's today's guide:

- **Types of Emotions:** Start by familiarizing yourself with different types of emotions. Emotions are complex, and there's a wide range of them. Common emotions include joy, sadness, anger, fear, surprise, and disgust. Take time to reflect on the specific emotions you've experienced recently.

- **Emotional Triggers:** Reflect on what triggers different emotions in your life. Emotions often arise in response to specific situations, thoughts, or events. Understanding your triggers is crucial for emotional intelligence.

- **Emotional Responses:** Consider how you typically respond to various emotions. Do you express them openly, or do you tend to suppress or hide them? Recognize any patterns in your emotional responses. Understanding how you react to emotions is an essential aspect of self-awareness.

- **Physiological Responses:** Emotions are not just psychological; they also manifest physically. Pay attention to how your body reacts when you experience different emotions.

- **Emotions and Behavior:** Reflect on how your emotions influence your behavior. Emotions can motivate actions, both positive and negative.

Consider times when your emotions have prompted you to take specific actions and assess the outcomes.

- **Emotions in Communication:** Think about how emotions play a role in your communication with others. Emotions often drive the way we express ourselves and interpret others' expressions.

- **Journaling:** Consider maintaining an emotions journal throughout the day. Record your emotions as they arise, along with the associated triggers, physical sensations, and any actions or behaviors they lead to.

- **Reflection:** Take time to reflect on what you've learned about your emotions today. What insights have you gained? Are there any patterns or recurring themes in your emotional experiences? How do these insights impact your understanding of yourself?

Day 1 sets the foundation for your journey in developing emotional intelligence. By comprehensively exploring your emotions, triggers, responses, and their impact, you gain a deeper understanding of yourself. This understanding is a vital step toward effectively managing your emotions and enhancing your overall emotional well-being.

Day 2 – Managing Emotions:

Today is dedicated to learning techniques for managing emotions constructively. Effective emotional management is a key component of emotional intelligence. This practice focuses on calming your mind and body when faced with strong emotions. Here's a comprehensive guide:

- **Deep Breathing Exercise:** Begin with a deep breathing exercise, a powerful technique to manage emotions. Find a quiet and comfortable place to sit or lie down. Close your eyes if it's comfortable for you. Take a moment to connect with your breath. Inhale slowly through your nose, counting to four as you do so. Feel your lungs fill with air, and allow your abdomen to expand as you breathe in deeply. Exhale slowly through your mouth, also counting to four. As you exhale, release any tension or stress you may be holding. Feel the breath leaving your body. Continue this deep breathing cycle for several minutes. Maintain your focus on your breath, allowing it to anchor you to the present moment. If your mind wanders, gently bring it back to your breath.

- **Progressive Muscle Relaxation:** After the deep breathing exercise, practice progressive muscle relaxation. Start with your toes and work your way up through your body. Tense each muscle group for a few seconds and then release, allowing them to relax completely. This technique helps release physical tension associated with strong emotions.

- **Mindful Acknowledgment:** While practicing deep breathing and muscle relaxation, acknowledge the emotions you're experiencing without judgment. Recognize that it's okay to feel these emotions; they are a natural part of being human.

- **Positive Self-Talk:** If you find yourself struggling with particularly challenging emotions, engage in positive self-talk. Challenge any negative self-perceptions or thoughts and replace them with affirmations that promote self-compassion and resilience.

- **Practice Regularly:** Emotion management is a skill that improves with practice. The more you practice, the more effective these strategies become.

- **Journaling:** Use your journal to track your emotional responses and the effectiveness of these techniques. Note the situations or triggers that led to strong emotions and how your management strategies helped you regain control.

- **Seek Support if Needed:** If you find that managing your emotions becomes overwhelming or consistently challenging, consider seeking support from a therapist or counselor.

Day 2 equips you with valuable tools for managing emotions effectively. These techniques help you regain control during moments of emotional intensity and promote emotional well-being. As you continue to practice emotion management, you'll develop a stronger sense of emotional intelligence, leading to healthier relationships with yourself and others.

Day 3 – Empathy Building:

Today's practice is dedicated to developing empathy, a crucial aspect of emotional intelligence. Empathy involves understanding and sharing the feelings of others, which fosters better connections and relationships. Here's a comprehensive guide:

- **Understanding Empathy:** Begin by gaining a clear understanding of what empathy is. Empathy is the ability to step into someone else's shoes, to see the world from their perspective, and to genuinely comprehend their feelings.

- **Active Listening:** Engage in conversations today where you actively listen to others. Choose a friend, family member, or colleague with whom you can have a meaningful dialogue. As they speak, focus on their words, tone, and body language.

- **Suspend Judgment:** Practice suspending judgment during the conversation. Avoid jumping to conclusions or making assumptions about the other person's feelings or experiences. Instead, strive to genuinely understand their viewpoint.

- **Ask Open-Ended Questions:** Encourage the other person to share more about their emotions and experiences by asking open-ended questions. These questions invite them to elaborate and express themselves fully.

- **Reflect Back:** Use reflective listening to convey that you understand and empathize with their emotions. Phrases like "I hear you," or "It sounds like you're feeling..." show that you're actively engaged and trying to comprehend their perspective.

- **Non-Verbal Cues:** Pay attention to non-verbal cues, such as facial expressions, gestures, and body language. These can offer valuable insights into the other person's emotions, which you can acknowledge and validate.

- **Empathetic Responses:** Respond to the other person's emotions with empathy and compassion. Express your understanding and support, letting them know that their feelings are valid and respected.

- **Reflect on Your Experience:** After the conversation, take time to reflect on your empathetic experience. Consider how actively listening and empathizing with the other person made you feel and how it may have impacted your relationship.

- **Practice Empathy Daily:** Make empathy a daily practice. Extend your empathetic listening skills to various interactions in your life, whether with loved ones, colleagues, or even strangers. The more you practice empathy, the more it becomes a natural part of your communication.

- **Self-Empathy:** Finally, remember to practice self-empathy. Understand and acknowledge your own emotions and experiences with the same level of compassion and understanding you offer to others. Self-empathy is fundamental to emotional intelligence.

By actively listening and empathizing, you not only strengthen your emotional intelligence but also foster deeper and more meaningful relationships in your personal and professional life.

Day 4 – Positive Self-Talk:

Cultivating positive self-talk is a crucial element of emotional intelligence. Positive self-talk involves challenging negative self-perceptions and replacing them with affirmations that promote self-compassion and resilience. Here's a comprehensive guide:

- **Understanding Self-Talk:** Start by understanding what self-talk is. Self-talk refers to the inner dialogue and thoughts that run through your mind throughout the day. These thoughts can be either positive or negative and greatly influence your emotions and behavior.

- **Identify Negative Self-Talk:** Pay attention to any negative or self-critical thoughts that arise during the day. These may include self-doubt, self-blame, or harsh self-judgments. Identifying negative thoughts is the first step in changing them.

- **Challenge Negative Beliefs:** When you recognize negative self-talk, challenge the beliefs underlying those thoughts. Ask yourself questions like, "Is this thought based on facts or assumptions?" or "Would I say this to a friend in a similar situation?"

- **Affirmations for Self-Compassion:** Replace negative self-talk with positive affirmations that promote self-compassion. For example, if you catch yourself thinking, "I'm not good enough," replace it with, "I am capable, and I'm doing my best."

- **Affirmations for Resilience:** Create affirmations that boost your resilience in the face of challenges. For instance, instead of thinking, "I can't handle this," tell yourself, "I am strong and capable of overcoming obstacles."

- **Repetition:** Repeat these affirmations regularly throughout the day. The more you repeat them, the more they become ingrained in your thinking patterns. Consistent positive self-talk can reshape your mindset over time.

- **Visualize Success:** Use visualization as a tool for positive self-talk. Imagine yourself succeeding in challenging situations. Visualization can enhance your confidence and motivation.

- **Externalize Negative Thoughts:** Sometimes, it helps to externalize negative thoughts by writing them down. Once on paper, you can objectively evaluate their accuracy and challenge them with more realistic and compassionate beliefs.

- **Create a Positive Mantra:** Develop a personal mantra or phrase that encapsulates your strengths and values. This mantra can serve as a powerful reminder of your worth and potential.

- **Self-Compassion:** Remember to treat yourself with kindness and self-compassion throughout this practice. Recognize that changing long-standing thought patterns takes time and effort. Be patient with yourself.

Positive self-talk empowers you to shift your internal dialogue in a more supportive and self-compassionate direction. By challenging negative beliefs and embracing positive affirmations, you'll enhance your emotional intelligence, boost self-esteem, and cultivate a more positive outlook on life.

Day 5 – Reflection and Application:

This is a day for reflection and application, allowing you to consolidate your understanding and practice of emotional intelligence principles throughout the week.

- **Morning Reflection:** Start your day with a few moments of reflection. Think back on the lessons and practices from the previous four days. What stood out to you?

- **Journaling:** If you've been keeping a journal throughout the week, review your entries. Take note of any patterns or changes in your emotional responses, your experiences with empathy, positive self-talk, and emotion management.

- **Moments of Success**: Identify moments during the week where you successfully managed your emotions, practiced empathy, or employed positive self-talk. These moments of success can serve as reminders of your growth.

- **Challenges Faced:** Reflect on any challenges or difficulties you encountered while applying emotional intelligence principles. Recognize that growth often comes with challenges, and acknowledging them is a crucial step toward improvement.

- **Impact on Relationships:** Consider how your practice of emotional intelligence impacted your relationships. Did you notice any changes in how you interacted with others or how they responded to you?

- **Self-Compassion:** Assess how practicing positive self-talk and self-compassion affected your self-esteem and self-perception. Did you find yourself more resilient in the face of self-doubt or criticism?

- **Emotion Management:** Reflect on instances when you effectively managed strong emotions. How did deep breathing and muscle relaxation techniques help you regain control? Did you notice reduced stress or increased emotional regulation?

- **Empathy Experiences:** Think about your experiences with empathy during conversations. Did you notice improved understanding of others' emotions? How did empathetic listening enhance your relationships?

- **Express Gratitude:** Close your reflection session by expressing gratitude for the growth and insights you've gained during the week. Acknowledge the effort you've put into nurturing your emotional well-being.

- **Share Your Experiences:** If you're participating in a group or program, consider sharing your experiences and reflections with others. Sharing can provide mutual support and inspire further growth.

Today's practice of focus on reflection and application helps you consolidate your understanding of emotional intelligence principles and their practical impact. By reflecting on your experiences and setting intentions for ongoing growth, you continue to develop your emotional intelligence, fostering healthier relationships with yourself and others.

During the past week, you embarked on a transformative journey, focusing on "Developing Emotional Intelligence." This week's practices were dedicated to understanding, managing, and harnessing the power of emotions effectively.

Throughout the week, you developed emotional intelligence skills that can lead to healthier relationships, both with yourself and others. By actively engaging in these practices, you not only gained insights into your emotions but also equipped yourself with valuable tools for navigating the complexities of the human emotional experience.

As you reflect on the past week, remember that emotional growth is an ongoing process. Continue to practice these techniques regularly, integrating them into your daily life. Emotional intelligence is a skill that can be honed and refined over time, ultimately leading to more meaningful connections and a deeper understanding of yourself.

Week 5: Stress Management Fundamentals:

Welcome to Week 5 of our "Mindful Living" journey. This week, we'll focus on the fundamentals of stress management. In today's fast-paced world, learning to manage stress is crucial for your overall well-being.

Day 1 – Understanding Stress:

Stress is a prevalent aspect of modern life, and being aware of its sources and effects is crucial for effective stress management. Here's a comprehensive guide:

- **What is Stress:** Begin by defining stress. Stress is the body's natural response to a perceived threat or challenge. It triggers a cascade of physiological and psychological reactions aimed at preparing you to cope with the situation.

- **Types of Stress:** Recognize that there are different types of stress. Acute stress is short-term and often linked to specific situations (e.g., a tight deadline). Chronic stress is prolonged and can result from ongoing life challenges (e.g., work-related stress or financial concerns).

- **Physical Symptoms:** Understand how stress manifests physically. Stress can lead to symptoms such as increased heart rate, muscle tension, shallow breathing, headaches, digestive issues, and a weakened immune system.

- **Emotional Impact:** Explore the emotional impact of stress. Stress can contribute to feelings of anxiety, irritability, sadness, or even anger. It can also affect your ability to concentrate and make decisions.

- **Common Stressors:** Identify common stressors in your life. These may include work-related pressures, relationship challenges, financial worries, health concerns, or major life changes. Recognizing these stressors is the first step in managing them.

- **Individual Responses:** Understand that each person responds to stress differently. What may be stressful for one person may not be the same for another. Your unique experiences, coping mechanisms, and support systems play a significant role in how you handle stress.

- **Impact on Well-being:** Reflect on how stress impacts your overall well-being. Stress can have long-term effects on your physical health, mental health, and relationships if left unmanaged.

- **Stress Awareness:** Throughout the day, practice stress awareness. Pay attention to moments when you feel stressed or overwhelmed. Recognize the signs and symptoms you experience when stress arises.

Today's focus on understanding stress lays the foundation for effective stress management. By becoming aware of the types of stress, its physical and emotional effects, and common stressors in your life, you empower yourself to take proactive steps in addressing and mitigating stress.

Day 2 – Deep Breathing Exercises:

Today is all about practicing deep breathing exercises, a simple yet powerful technique to instantly reduce stress. Deep breathing can help calm the nervous system, reduce tension, and promote relaxation. Here's a comprehensive guide:

- **Understanding Deep Breathing:** Begin by understanding the importance of deep breathing. Deep breathing involves taking slow, deliberate breaths that fully engage your diaphragm. This technique counters shallow, rapid breathing associated with stress.

- **Preparation:** Find a quiet and comfortable place where you won't be disturbed. Sit or lie down in a relaxed position. Place one hand on your chest and the other on your abdomen to monitor your breath.

- **Four-Four-Four Technique:** Practice the "Four-Four-Four" deep breathing technique. Inhale deeply through your nose for a count of four seconds. Feel your abdomen expand as you fill your lungs with air.

- **Hold the Breath:** After inhaling, hold your breath for another count of four seconds. This brief pause allows your body to absorb the oxygen and prepares you for the exhale.

- **Exhale Slowly:** Exhale slowly and completely through your mouth for a count of four seconds. Focus on releasing tension as you breathe out.

- **Repeat:** Continue this "Four-Four-Four" deep breathing pattern for several minutes. You can gradually extend the duration of each phase if you feel comfortable doing so. The key is to maintain a slow and rhythmic breathing pattern.

- **Mindful Focus:** As you practice deep breathing, maintain your focus on the breath. Pay attention to the sensation of the air entering and leaving your body. If your mind wanders, gently bring your attention back to your breath.

- **Daily Integration:** Incorporate deep breathing exercises into your daily routine. You can practice them whenever you feel stressed, anxious, or in need of relaxation. It's a portable stress-reduction tool you can use anywhere.

- **Stress Response:** Understand that deep breathing triggers the body's relaxation response. It reduces the production of stress hormones, lowers heart rate, and promotes a sense of calm and well-being.

- **Variations:** Explore different deep breathing variations, such as diaphragmatic breathing or the 4-7-8 technique, to find the one that resonates best with you.

Day 2's practice of deep breathing provides you with a valuable tool for managing stress in your daily life. By mastering this technique, you can instantly reduce stress levels and promote relaxation whenever needed. Deep breathing is a fundamental skill that complements other stress management strategies.

Day 3 – Progressive Muscle Relaxation:

Today, we will employ progressive muscle relaxation techniques, an effective method for releasing physical tension and stress from your body. This practice involves systematically tensing and then relaxing different muscle groups to promote relaxation and reduce stress.

- **Understanding Progressive Muscle Relaxation:** Start by understanding the concept of progressive muscle relaxation (PMR). PMR is a relaxation technique that involves intentionally tensing and then relaxing specific muscle groups to reduce physical tension and stress.

- **Preparation:** Find a quiet and comfortable place where you can sit or lie down. Ensure you won't be disturbed during this practice. Loosen any tight clothing and get into a relaxed position.

- **Breathing Awareness:** Begin with a few deep breaths to settle in and bring your attention to the present moment. Breathe in deeply through your nose and exhale slowly through your mouth.

- **Tension Phase:** Focus on one muscle group at a time, starting with your toes. As you breathe in, deliberately tense the muscle group as much as you can without straining. Hold the tension for a few seconds (around 5-10 seconds).

- **Release Phase:** As you exhale, release the tension in that muscle group completely. Allow the muscles to relax fully. Pay attention to the sensation of relaxation and the contrast between tension and relaxation.

- **Progressive Sequence:** Progress through different muscle groups in a systematic order. Move from your toes to your feet, ankles, calves, thighs, buttocks, abdomen, chest, back, shoulders, arms, hands, neck, and finally, your face. Take your time with each group.

- **Mindful Focus:** Throughout the practice, maintain mindful awareness of the sensations in each muscle group. Notice the difference between tension and relaxation. If your mind wanders, gently bring your focus back to the muscles.

- **Release Tension:** Use each exhalation as an opportunity to release any remaining tension from the muscle group you're working on. Feel the stress melting away with each breath.

- **Complete Relaxation:** Once you've gone through all muscle groups, take a few minutes to enjoy the deep sense of relaxation that has washed over your entire body. Bask in the feelings of tranquility and calm.

The routine practice of progressive muscle relaxation provides you with a valuable tool for reducing physical tension and promoting relaxation. By systematically working through muscle groups and releasing tension, you'll not only experience physical relief but also improve your overall stress management skills.

Day 4 – Nature Connection:

Connect with the natural world to find solace and calm. Take time to immerse yourself in nature, disconnect from technology, and embrace the beauty of the outdoors. This practice can be a soothing balm for stress and a source of inspiration.

- **Nature Retreat:** Dedicate time to connect with nature. Whether it's a leisurely walk in the park, a hike in the woods, or simply spending a few moments in your garden, allow nature to be your sanctuary.

- **Mindful Observation:** As you immerse yourself in nature, practice mindful observation. Pay attention to the sights, sounds, and sensations around you. Notice the details of plants, trees, and wildlife.

- **Deep Breathing:** Combine your nature experience with deep breathing. Inhale the fresh outdoor air deeply, and as you exhale, let go of stress and tension. Nature can have a soothing effect on your mind.

- **Disconnect from Technology:** During your nature time, disconnect from electronic devices. Put away your phone and other distractions to fully engage with the natural world.

- **Presence and Appreciation:** Be present in the moment and appreciate the beauty of nature. Notice the colors, textures, and the way sunlight filters through leaves. Allow yourself to feel a sense of wonder and awe.

- **Mindful Walking:** If you're walking in nature, practice mindful walking. Feel the earth beneath your feet, the gentle sway of branches, and the rustling of leaves. Be fully engaged with each step.

- **Nature Sounds:** Listen to the sounds of nature. The chirping of birds, the babbling of a stream, or the wind in the trees can have a calming and grounding effect.

- **Relaxation:** Use this time in nature as an opportunity for relaxation and stress relief. Let go of worries and concerns, and simply exist in the natural environment.

- **Gratitude:** Express gratitude for the beauty and serenity of nature. Consider how it makes you feel and the sense of calm it brings. Gratitude can enhance your connection to the natural world.

- **Regular Practice:** Make nature connection a regular part of your routine. Even brief moments in nature can provide significant mental and emotional benefits. Incorporating it into your life can contribute to ongoing stress management.

The practice of connecting with nature allows you to find solace and tranquility in the natural world. Whether through mindful observation, deep breathing, or simply being present, nature can serve as a powerful antidote to stress and a source of inspiration and rejuvenation.

Day 5 – Stress Reduction Techniques:

On this day, we embark on an exploration of various stress reduction techniques. It's a chance to discover what resonates with you and empowers you to effectively manage stress. Embrace these practices, and let them guide you toward a more serene and balanced life.

- **Exploration:** Dedicate time to explore various stress reduction techniques. Stress management is not one-size-fits-all, so be open to trying different methods.

- **Meditation:** Begin with meditation. Find a quiet place to sit comfortably, close your eyes, and focus on your breath. Meditation can calm your mind and reduce stress.

- **Mindfulness:** Practice mindfulness exercises. Be fully present in the moment, whether it's during daily activities or through mindful breathing.

- **Yoga:** Explore yoga for stress reduction. Engage in gentle yoga poses and stretches while paying attention to your breath and body.

- **Progressive Muscle Relaxation:** Revisit progressive muscle relaxation. Tense and release muscle groups to release physical tension.

- **Nature Connection:** Reflect on the benefits of connecting with nature and consider making it a regular part of your routine for stress relief.

- **Journaling:** Continue journaling about your experiences and insights from this week's stress management practices. Journaling can enhance self-awareness.

- **Customization:** Recognize that what works best for stress reduction may vary from person to person. Customize your approach based on your preferences and needs.

- **Consistency:** Stress management is most effective when practiced consistently. Incorporate these techniques into your daily or weekly routine for lasting benefits.

- **Self-Care:** Remember the importance of self-care. Prioritize activities that promote relaxation and well-being in your daily life.

I wholeheartedly encourage you to embark on a journey of exploration when it comes to stress reduction techniques.

By customizing these practices to align with your daily rhythm and preferences, you empower yourself with the ability to manage stress effectively. Stress is a part of life, but with these tools in hand, you can transform how you respond to it.

As you do, you'll not only navigate life's challenges with grace but also enhance your overall well-being, embracing each day with renewed energy and a sense of inner peace. So, go forth with confidence, for this journey is your path to a more vibrant, balanced, and fulfilled life

During this week of Stress Management Fundamentals, we embarked on a transformative journey toward greater resilience and inner calm. Each day offered invaluable insights and tools to navigate life's challenges with grace.

Throughout this week, we gained essential skills for recognizing and managing stress effectively. By incorporating these practices into our daily lives, we now stand better equipped to navigate life's challenges with resilience and a newfound sense of inner peace. The journey we've embarked upon is not merely about managing stress; it's a profound transformation of how we relate to stressors, empowering us to respond with grace and wisdom.

As we look ahead to Week 6, be prepared to delve even deeper into the art of stress management. Advanced Stress Management Strategies await us, promising to refine our skills, enhance our emotional resilience, and equip us with advanced tools to thrive in the face of life's complexities. Join us as we continue this empowering journey toward a life marked by calm and mastery over stress, ready to face each day with renewed vigor and a sense of balance.

Week 6: Stress Management Strategies:

Welcome to Week 6 of our "Mindful Living" journey. This week, we'll delve into more advanced stress relief practices to help you further manage stress and foster resilience.

Day 1 – Creative Outlets:

Creative expression can be a powerful tool for relieving stress and enhancing your overall well-being. Today, we encourage you to engage in creative activities that allow you to tap into your inner artist. Here's how to do it:

- **Choose Your Creative Outlet**: Begin by selecting a creative activity that resonates with you. It could be painting, drawing, writing, playing a musical instrument, crafting, or any other form of creative expression that brings you joy and relaxation.

- **Create a Calm Space:** Find a quiet and comfortable space where you can fully immerse yourself in your chosen creative activity.

- **Let Go of Expectations:** Remember that the goal here is not to create a masterpiece but to release stress and nurture your creativity. Let go of any expectations or self-judgment. Embrace the process rather than focusing on the end result.

- **Begin with an Open Mind:** Start your creative session with an open and curious mind. Allow yourself to explore and experiment freely. There are no right or wrong ways to express yourself creatively.

- **Embrace Mindfulness:** As you engage in your creative activity, practice mindfulness. Pay attention to the sensations, colors, and textures involved. Let your mind become fully absorbed in the process, letting go of external worries and stressors.

- **Express Your Emotions:** Use your chosen creative outlet as a means to express your emotions. If you're feeling stressed, let that emotion flow into your creation.

- **Enjoy the Process:** Savor each moment of the creative process. Whether you're painting strokes on a canvas, writing words on a page, or playing notes on an instrument, find joy in the act of creation itself.

- **Reflect and Relax:** After your creative session, take a moment to reflect on how you feel. Notice if there's a sense of relief or relaxation. Creative outlets can offer a unique form of therapy that eases stress and fosters a sense of accomplishment.

- **Make it a Habit:** Consider making creative expression a regular part of your self-care routine. Set aside time each week to engage in your chosen creative activity. The more you practice, the more you'll reap the stress-relief benefits.

By incorporating creative outlets into your life, you provide yourself with a constructive and enjoyable way to cope with stress. Through the act of creation, you not only release tension but also tap into your inner creativity, fostering a sense of fulfillment and well-being. Enjoy the process, and let your creative journey be a source of solace and joy.

Day 2 – Technology Detox:

In our modern, technology-driven world, taking a break from screens and digital distractions can be a refreshing way to reduce stress and reconnect with simpler pleasures. Here's how to embark on a technology detox:

- **Choose Your Tech-Free Day:** Select a day when you can commit to disconnecting from screens. It could be a weekend or a day off from work when you have more flexibility.

- **Notify Others (If Necessary):** If you have work or personal commitments that typically involve technology, inform colleagues, friends, or family members in advance that you'll be unplugging for the day. Set expectations for your temporary absence.

- **Turn Off Devices:** Power down all your electronic devices, including smartphones, tablets, computers, and even your TV. Make sure they're out of sight and reach to minimize temptation.

- **Unplug from Social Media:** Log out of your social media accounts on any remaining devices. This step prevents you from absentmindedly checking updates.

- **Create a Tech-Free Environment:** Designate specific tech-free zones in your home where you can relax without digital distractions. Create a cozy corner for reading, meditating, or simply enjoying the peace and quiet.

- **Reconnect with Analog Pleasures:** Use this day to rediscover analog activities. Read a physical book, take a leisurely walk in nature, engage in face-to-face conversations, or enjoy hobbies that don't involve screens.

- **Mindful Observation:** While you're tech-free, practice mindful observation. Pay attention to the world around you, noticing the details you might usually overlook—the rustling of leaves, the colors of flowers, or the sounds of birds.

- **Journal Your Experience:** Keep a journal throughout the day to document your thoughts and feelings. Reflect on how the technology detox affects your stress levels and overall well-being.

- **Embrace Simplicity:** Embrace the simplicity of the day. Instead of constant notifications and information overload, savor the slower pace and serenity that a tech-free day can provide.

- **Evaluate the Impact:** At the end of the day, evaluate how the technology detox made you feel. Did it reduce stress? Did you enjoy the break from screens? Consider incorporating tech-free days into your routine on a regular basis.

A technology detox offers a chance to disconnect from the digital world and reconnect with the analog pleasures of life. It's an opportunity to de-stress, gain perspective, and appreciate the simple joys that often go unnoticed in our fast-paced, tech-savvy lives. Embrace this practice as a valuable self-care tool in your ongoing journey toward stress management and well-being.

Day 3 – Gentle Physical Exercise:

Incorporating gentle physical exercise into your routine can be a wonderful way to reduce stress, enhance physical well-being, and promote overall relaxation. Here's how to embrace this practice:

- **Choose Your Gentle Exercise:** Begin by selecting a gentle form of exercise that resonates with you. Yoga and Tai Chi are excellent options for promoting relaxation. These practices prioritize gentle, flowing movements and mindfulness.

- **Find a Suitable Space:** Locate a quiet and comfortable space where you can engage in your chosen exercise. Clear enough room to move freely without any obstructions.

- **Dress Comfortably:** Wear comfortable clothing that allows for unrestricted movement. Being at ease in your attire can enhance the relaxation experience.

- **Warm-Up:** Start with a gentle warm-up to prepare your body for exercise. Simple stretches and deep breaths can help you ease into the practice.

- **Follow a Guided Session (Optional):** If you're new to yoga or Tai Chi, consider following a guided session, either in-person or through online videos. There are many resources available for practitioners of all levels.

- **Mindful Movement:** As you engage in your chosen exercise, prioritize mindful movement. Pay attention to each movement and the sensations in your body. Let your mind stay fully present in the practice, releasing thoughts of stress and worries.

- **Breathing Awareness:** Focus on your breath throughout the exercise. Inhale deeply and exhale slowly, syncing your breath with your movements. This conscious breathing enhances relaxation and calms the mind.

- **Embrace Stillness:** Many gentle exercises incorporate moments of stillness or meditation. Embrace these moments, allowing your body and mind to find tranquility.

- **Savor the Experience:** Whether you're stretching, balancing, or flowing through movements, savor the experience. Notice how your body feels as it becomes more relaxed and supple.

- **Cool Down and Rest:** Conclude your gentle exercise with a cool-down period and rest. Lie down in Savasana (corpse pose) in yoga, or simply sit quietly in a state of relaxation, appreciating the sense of calm that gentle exercise has provided.

- **Regular Practice:** Consider making gentle exercise a regular part of your routine. Even a short session a few times a week can significantly contribute to stress reduction and physical well-being.

Gentle physical exercise serves as a nurturing practice that not only enhances your physical flexibility and strength but also cultivates a profound sense of relaxation. By prioritizing mindful movement and conscious breathing, you create a harmonious connection between your body and mind, fostering a state of tranquility and well-being. Enjoy this practice as a valuable tool in your ongoing journey toward stress management and self-care.

Day 4 – Mindful Relaxation:

On this day, we will explore advanced mindfulness and relaxation exercises to take your relaxation experience to a deeper level. Here's how to practice mindful relaxation:

- **Find a Tranquil Space:** Begin by locating a peaceful and comfortable space where you can fully relax without interruptions. Ensure that the environment promotes a sense of serenity.

- **Comfortable Posture:** Sit or lie down in a comfortable posture. You can choose to sit on a chair or cushion with your back straight but not rigid. Alternatively, lie down with your arms by your sides and your legs uncrossed.

- **Guided Meditation (Optional):** If you're new to mindfulness and relaxation, consider using guided meditation. There are numerous apps and online resources that offer guided sessions tailored to deep relaxation.

- **Mindful Body Scan:** Start with a body scan meditation. Begin at the top of your head and gradually move your attention down through your body. Notice any areas of tension or discomfort and release them as you breathe out.

- **Deep Breathing:** Focus on your breath. Inhale slowly through your nose, counting to four. Feel the breath fill your lungs, expand your chest and abdomen. Exhale gradually through your mouth for a count of four, letting go of any tension or stress with each breath.

- **Progressive Relaxation:** If tension persists, practice progressive muscle relaxation. Tense and release each muscle group in your body, starting from your toes and working your way up to your head.

- **Focus on the Present:** Bring your awareness to the present moment. Let go of thoughts about the past or future. Instead, immerse yourself in the here and now.

- **Embrace Silence:** Allow for moments of silence and stillness. Let your mind rest and be at peace without the need for constant thinking.

- **Gratitude:** Before concluding your mindful relaxation session, take a moment to express gratitude for this time you've dedicated to self-care and relaxation.

- **Gradual Awakening:** When you're ready to conclude, gradually awaken your body and mind. Slowly open your eyes if they were closed and gently move your fingers and toes.

- **Reflect:** After your mindful relaxation session, take a moment to reflect on how you feel. Notice any changes in your sense of calm and relaxation. Consider making mindful relaxation a regular part of your routine.

By practicing mindful relaxation, you can deepen your relaxation experience and find solace in the present moment. This practice allows you to release tension, calm your mind, and foster a profound sense of inner peace. Embrace it as a valuable tool in your ongoing journey toward stress management and self-care.

Day 5 – Stress Relief Plan:

Today, we will focus on developing a personalized stress relief plan that combines the techniques you've learned throughout the week. This plan will serve as your toolkit for managing stress effectively in various situations. Here's how to create your stress relief plan:

- **Reflect on the Week:** Begin by reflecting on the stress management techniques you've practiced throughout the week. Take a moment to acknowledge which ones resonated with you the most and had the greatest impact on reducing your stress.

- **Identify Your Stressors:** List the common stressors in your life. These could be work-related, personal, or environmental stressors. Recognizing your stress triggers is the first step in addressing them.

- **Choose Your Techniques:** Based on your reflections and the techniques you've practiced, select the stress management techniques that work best for you. These can include deep breathing, mindful relaxation, gentle physical exercise, or creative outlets.

- **Customize Your Toolkit:** Tailor your stress relief plan to suit your unique needs. Consider when and how you will implement each technique. For example, you might use deep breathing during a stressful meeting or engage in creative outlets when you need an emotional release.

- **Create a Routine:** Establish a routine for incorporating these techniques into your daily life. Whether it's dedicating time each morning for mindfulness exercises or having a creative session once a week, consistency is key.

- **Include Mindful Practices:** Ensure that mindfulness practices are an integral part of your toolkit. Mindfulness not only helps in managing stress but also enhances your overall well-being and resilience.

- **Set Realistic Goals:** Set achievable goals for managing stress. It's essential to be realistic about what you can accomplish and to be gentle with yourself if you have setbacks.

- **Monitor Progress:** Regularly assess how well your stress relief plan is working for you. Make adjustments as needed, and be open to trying new techniques or refining existing ones.

- **Practice Self-Care:** Remember that self-care is a vital component of stress management. Ensure you're getting enough rest, maintaining a healthy diet, and engaging in activities that bring you joy and relaxation.

- **Stay Committed:** Finally, commit to prioritizing your stress relief plan. Make it a non-negotiable part of your self-care routine. Your well-being is worth the effort.

By creating a personalized stress relief plan, you empower yourself with the tools and strategies needed to manage stress effectively. This plan is your roadmap to a calmer, more resilient you. Embrace it as a valuable resource in your ongoing journey toward stress management and well-being.

During this past week, you embarked on a journey of discovering effective stress management strategies, each day offering you new insights and tools for enhancing your well-being. Let's review the practices of "Stress Management Strategies":

As you progressed through this week, you discovered new ways to cope with stress and promote your mental and emotional resilience. By integrating these advanced strategies into your self-care routine, you've become better equipped to navigate life's challenges with grace and composure.

Stay tuned for Week 7, where we'll delve into the essential practices of self-compassion and self-love. These practices will deepen your connection with yourself and foster a kinder, more nurturing relationship with your inner world, further enhancing your overall well-being.

Week 7: Self-Compassion and Self-Love:

Welcome to Week 7 of our "Mindful Living" journey. This week, we'll focus on the importance of self-compassion and self-love in nurturing your well-being and maintaining a balanced life.

Day 1 – Self-Care Rituals:

Today, we begin by establishing daily self-care rituals that will nurture your well-being and reinforce your sense of self-worth. Here's how to cultivate self-compassion through self-care rituals:

- **Morning Ritual:** Start your day with a self-care ritual that sets a positive tone. This could be as simple as taking a few moments for deep breathing, gentle stretching, or morning affirmations. Choose practices that resonate with you and make you feel nurtured and valued.

- **Affirmations:** Incorporate positive affirmations into your morning routine. These are short, uplifting statements that reinforce your self-worth and self-compassion. For example, you might say, "I am worthy of love and care," or "I am enough just as I am." Repeat these affirmations with sincerity.

- **Mindful Moments:** Throughout the day, create mindful moments of self-care. Pause and check in with yourself. Ask how you're feeling emotionally and physically. Adjust your self-care rituals to meet your current needs. Whether it's a few deep breaths, a brief meditation, or a mindful walk, prioritize these moments of self-nurturing.

- **Evening Reflection:** At the end of the day, reflect on your self-care rituals and affirmations. Consider how they've impacted your emotional well-being. Express gratitude for the time and care you've devoted to yourself.

- **Consistency:** Make self-care rituals a consistent part of your daily routine. Consistency reinforces the message that you are deserving of love, care, and compassion.

- **Adapt and Evolve:** Be flexible in your self-care practices. As you explore self-compassion and self-love, you may discover new rituals that resonate with you. Be open to adapting and evolving your self-care routine.

- **Self-Kindness:** Approach yourself with kindness and understanding. If you miss a self-care ritual or have a challenging day, practice self-compassion. Remember that you are on a journey of nurturing your well-being.

By establishing daily self-care rituals, you're taking a significant step towards fostering self-compassion and self-love. These practices will not only enhance your emotional well-being but also strengthen your resilience. Embrace this week as an opportunity to deepen your connection with yourself and prioritize self-care as an essential part of your life.

Day 2 – Setting Healthy Boundaries

Today, we will delve into the importance of setting healthy boundaries. Boundaries are essential for safeguarding your emotional well-being and fostering self-compassion. Here's how to practice the art of setting healthy boundaries:

- **Self-Reflection**: Begin by reflecting on areas in your life where you may need to establish or reinforce boundaries. Consider situations, relationships, or commitments that have previously caused you emotional distress or drained your energy.

- **Identify Boundaries:** Clearly define the boundaries you wish to establish. These boundaries can involve your personal space, time, emotional energy, or any aspect of your life where you feel the need for protection.

- **Communicate Your Boundaries:** When appropriate, communicate your boundaries to those who need to be aware of them. Express your needs and expectations kindly but firmly. Remember that setting boundaries is an act of self-respect, not selfishness.

- **Practice Assertiveness:** Embrace assertiveness as a means of upholding your boundaries. Assertiveness involves respectfully standing up for your needs and values while considering the needs of others. It's a valuable skill for maintaining emotional balance.

- **Prioritize Self-Care:** Setting healthy boundaries often means prioritizing self-care. Allocate time for self-nurturing practices and ensure that you don't overcommit or spread yourself too thin.

- **Listen to Your Intuition:** Tune into your intuition and emotions. They can serve as powerful guides in recognizing when a boundary has been crossed or when it's time to set a new one.

- **Be Consistent:** Consistency is key in maintaining healthy boundaries. Stick to your boundaries even when it may be challenging. Consistency reinforces your commitment.

- **Respect Others' Boundaries:** Just as you set boundaries for yourself, respect the boundaries of others. Mutual respect fosters healthier relationships and emotional well-being.

- **Self-Compassion:** Practice self-compassion throughout this process. Understand that setting boundaries is an act of self-love and protection, not a rejection of others. You deserve to prioritize your emotional well-being.

By embracing the practice of setting healthy boundaries, you empower yourself to protect your emotional well-being and cultivate self-compassion. These boundaries are a form of self-care that allows you to maintain healthier relationships, reduce emotional stress, and honor your own needs. As you progress through this week, remember that self-compassion includes valuing yourself enough to create and maintain boundaries that promote your overall well-being.

Day 3 – Self-Love Affirmations:

Let's continue to focus on self-compassion and self-love. Today, we explore the powerful practice of self-love affirmations, which can enhance your sense of self-worth and self-compassion. Here's how to cultivate self-love through affirmations:

- **Choose Affirmations:** Begin by selecting self-love affirmations that resonate with you. These are positive statements that reflect your inherent worth, self-compassion, and self-acceptance. Some examples include, "I am worthy of love and respect," or "I am enough just as I am."

- **Repeat with Conviction:** Find a quiet and comfortable space to sit or stand. Close your eyes and take a few deep breaths to center yourself. As you repeat your chosen affirmations, say them with conviction and sincerity. Feel their truth resonate within you.

- **Practice Regularly:** Make self-love affirmations a regular part of your daily routine. You can repeat them in the morning, throughout the day, or before bedtime. Consistency reinforces their positive impact.

- **Use Mirrors:** For added effectiveness, practice self-love affirmations in front of a mirror. Look into your own eyes as you say the affirmations, connecting with yourself on a deeper level.

- **Challenge Negative Thoughts:** Whenever negative self-talk arises, counter it with your self-love affirmations. Use them as a tool to challenge and replace critical or self-doubting thoughts.

- **Write Them Down:** Consider writing down your self-love affirmations in a journal or on sticky notes placed where you'll see them frequently. Visual reminders can reinforce their positive messages.

- **Reflect on Progress:** At the end of the day, reflect on how practicing self-love affirmations affected your emotional well-being. Notice any shifts in your self-perception and self-compassion.

- **Adjust and Expand:** Over time, adjust your affirmations to reflect your evolving self-compassion and self-love journey. Add new affirmations or modify existing ones as needed.

- **Self-Kindness:** Approach yourself with kindness and patience throughout this practice. Understand that self-love is an ongoing process, and it's natural to have moments of self-doubt.

- **Embrace Self-Compassion:** As you repeat self-love affirmations, embrace the warmth of self-compassion. These affirmations are a daily reminder that you are deserving of love, care, and respect.

By incorporating self-love affirmations into your daily life, you actively nurture your sense of self-worth and self-compassion. These affirmations serve as a constant reminder that you are enough and deserving of love. As you progress through this week, allow self-love to become an integral part of your inner dialogue, fostering emotional well-being and a deeper connection with yourself.

Day 4 – Gratitude and Appreciation:

We continue our exploration of self-love and self-compassion. Today's practice focuses on expressing gratitude and appreciation for yourself, reinforcing your self-worth. Here's how to nurture self-love through gratitude and appreciation:

- **Set Aside Quiet Time:** Begin by setting aside some quiet and uninterrupted time for yourself. Find a comfortable space where you won't be disturbed.
- **Reflect on Qualities:** Take a moment to reflect on your qualities, achievements, and the things you love about yourself. These can be related to your personality, talents, accomplishments, or any other aspects that make you unique.
- **Write a Gratitude List:** Grab a journal or a piece of paper, and start writing a gratitude list dedicated to yourself. Write down the qualities and aspects of yourself that you're grateful for. For example, "I'm grateful for my resilience," or "I appreciate my kindness."
- **Reflect on Achievements:** Consider your achievements, no matter how big or small they may seem. Acknowledge the efforts and determination that led to these accomplishments.

- **Self-Love Letter:** Write a heartfelt letter to yourself, expressing your gratitude and appreciation. Address it as if you're writing to a dear friend. Mention specific qualities and experiences that make you proud of who you are.

- **Visual Reminders:** If you prefer visual cues, create a vision board or collage with images and words that represent your self-love, qualities, and achievements. Place it where you can see it daily.

- **Daily Affirmations:** Transform some of your gratitude statements into daily self-love affirmations. Repeat them regularly to reinforce your self-worth.

- **Share Your Gratitude:** If you feel comfortable, share your gratitude and self-appreciation with a trusted friend or family member. Sharing your journey can deepen your connection with others.

- **Self-Celebration:** Celebrate yourself by treating yourself to a small indulgence or self-care activity that brings joy. This is a way of physically manifesting your self-love.

- **Repeat and Reflect:** Continue this practice regularly, reflecting on your gratitude and appreciation for yourself. Allow it to become a natural part of your self-love journey.

By acknowledging and expressing gratitude and appreciation for yourself, you reinforce your self-worth and self-love. This practice helps you recognize and celebrate your unique qualities and achievements, fostering emotional well-being and self-compassion. As you progress through this week, may self-love continue to grow within you, strengthening your emotional resilience and deepening your connection with yourself.

Day 5 – Acts of Kindness:

I want to emphasize the importance of self-compassion and self-love. Today's practice involves performing acts of kindness toward yourself, reinforcing your sense of self-worth. Here's how to cultivate self-love through acts of kindness:

- **Self-Care Activity:** Begin by selecting a self-care activity or indulgence that brings you joy and comfort. It could be something as simple as taking a soothing bath, reading a book, or enjoying a favorite treat.

- **Dedicate Time:** Set aside a specific time in your day to engage in this self-care activity. Ensure that you have enough time to fully enjoy and immerse yourself in the experience.

- **Mindful Presence:** As you engage in your chosen self-care activity, practice mindful presence. Focus on the sensations, emotions, and thoughts that arise during this time. Be fully present in the moment.

- **Self-Kindness:** Throughout the activity, be kind and compassionate toward yourself. Recognize that you deserve this moment of self-indulgence and relaxation. Avoid self-criticism or guilt.

- **Reflect on Self-Worth**: While indulging in self-care, reflect on your self-worth. Consider the reasons why you are deserving of this act of kindness. Recognize your inherent value as a person.

- **Gratitude:** Express gratitude for yourself during this time. Think about the qualities and experiences that make you grateful for who you are. Feel appreciation for your self-worth.

- **Unplug and Disconnect:** If possible, disconnect from digital distractions during your self-care activity. This allows you to fully immerse yourself in the experience without external interruptions.

- **Repeat Regularly:** Make acts of kindness toward yourself a regular practice. Dedicate time to self-care and self-indulgence, reinforcing your self-love and self-compassion.

- **Journal Your Experience:** After each self-care session, consider journaling about your experience. Write down your thoughts and emotions, as well as any insights or moments of self-compassion that arose during the practice.

- **Share Your Journey:** If you feel comfortable, share your self-love journey and acts of kindness with a trusted friend or family member. Sharing your experience can deepen your connection with others.

By engaging in acts of kindness and self-care, you actively nurture your self-love and self-compassion. These practices serve as a tangible way to reinforce your self-worth and prioritize your emotional well-being. As you progress through this week, may self-love continue to flourish within you, promoting emotional resilience and a deeper connection with yourself.

Each day brought a unique practice that encouraged a deeper connection with ourselves and emphasized the significance of self-compassion and self-love in nurturing our emotional well-being.

Stay Tuned for Week 8 - Integration and Holistic Self-Care: In Week 8, we'll explore the theme of "Integration and Holistic Self-Care." This week will guide us in integrating the practices we've learned so far into our daily lives, fostering a sense of wholeness and balance. Join us as we continue this transformative journey toward well-being and self-discovery.

Week 8: Integration and Holistic Self-Care:

Welcome to Week 8 of our "Mindful Living" journey. This week, we'll bring together the practices from previous weeks, emphasizing the importance of a holistic self-care routine that nurtures your physical, mental, and emotional well-being.

Day 1 – Holistic Self-Care Assessment:

We begin by conducting a thorough assessment of our self-care practices.

- **Self-Reflection:** Start by finding a quiet and comfortable space where you can reflect on your self-care practices without distractions.

- **Inventory of Current Practices:** Take a moment to list down your current self-care practices. These may include mindfulness exercises, physical activities, emotional awareness practices, stress management techniques, and self-love rituals. Include any practices you engage in regularly.

- **Identify Strengths and Weaknesses:** Review your list and identify areas where you excel in self-care. These could be practices that you consistently prioritize and find particularly beneficial. Celebrate your strengths and recognize what you're doing well.

- **Recognize Gaps and Areas for Improvement:** Next, identify gaps in your self-care routine or areas where you might be neglecting your well-being. These could be practices that you've wanted to incorporate but haven't, or aspects of self-care that you've overlooked.

- **Prioritize Goals:** Based on your assessment, prioritize self-care goals for improvement. Choose one or two areas where you'd like to enhance your self-care practices. These goals should align with your overall well-being and resonate with your needs.

- **Action Plan:** Create a practical action plan to address the identified areas for improvement. Set clear and achievable goals for incorporating new self-care practices. Determine the specific steps you'll take to reach these goals.

- **Schedule and Commitment:** Allocate time in your daily or weekly schedule to implement these changes. Make a commitment to yourself to prioritize self-care and hold yourself accountable.

- **Evaluation and Adaptation:** Regularly evaluate your progress in implementing your self-care goals. Be open to adaptation and refinement as you discover what works best for you. Celebrate your successes along the way, no matter how small they may seem.

By conducting a holistic self-care assessment, you gain a comprehensive understanding of your self-care practices, strengths, and areas for improvement. This foundational step sets the stage for a well-rounded and balanced self-care routine that nurtures your physical, mental, and emotional well-being. It's a powerful way to start Week 8 on the path to holistic self-care.

Day 2 – Creating a Balanced Routine:

Welcome to Day 2 of Week 8, where we'll focus on creating a balanced daily self-care routine that integrates various aspects of holistic self-care. This routine will be tailored to your unique needs and goals, ensuring that you're nurturing your physical, mental, and emotional well-being effectively.

- **Self-Reflection:** Begin by taking a moment for self-reflection. Consider your current daily routine and how you typically spend your time.

- **Identify Priorities:** Identify the areas of your life that require more attention and care. These could be related to your mental health, physical fitness, emotional well-being, or any other aspect of your life that you value.

- **Set Clear Intentions:** Determine your intentions for your self-care routine. What do you want to achieve through your daily self-care practices? Clarify your objectives and what success looks like for you.

- **Mindfulness Integration:** Incorporate mindfulness into your routine. Allocate time for mindfulness practices such as meditation, deep breathing exercises, or mindful journaling. These practices enhance mental clarity and emotional balance.

- **Emotional Wellness Practices:** Devote time to emotional wellness. Continue journaling and expressing gratitude, which helps maintain emotional awareness. Consider incorporating practices like positive affirmations to reinforce self-compassion and self-love.

- **Balancing Physical Well-Being:** Prioritize physical well-being by including activities that promote both fitness and relaxation. This could involve gentle exercise, yoga, stretching, or a leisurely walk.

- **Adaptability:** Ensure your routine is adaptable to different days and situations. Some days, you might have more time for self-care, while others may be busier. Adapt your routine as needed without feeling pressured.

- **Consistency:** Commit to your daily self-care routine with consistency. The more you integrate these practices into your life, the more profound their effects will be.

- **Self-Compassion:** Remember that your self-care routine is a form of self-compassion. Treat yourself with kindness and understanding, especially if you encounter setbacks or challenges along the way.

- **Review and Adapt:** Periodically review your self-care routine to ensure it aligns with your evolving needs and goals. Adapt and refine it as necessary to continue nurturing your holistic well-being effectively.

Creating a balanced self-care routine that integrates mindfulness, emotional wellness, physical well-being, and adaptability is a powerful way to nurture your overall well-being. This practice empowers you to maintain equilibrium in your life while embracing the holistic approach to self-care.

Day 3 – Mind-Body Connection:

Today, we will explore the profound connection between your mind and body. Engaging in physical activities that promote mental clarity and well-being is the focus of today's practice.

- **Understanding the Mind-Body Connection:** Begin by understanding the intricate link between your mind and body. Recognize that the state of your mind can significantly influence your physical well-being, and visa versa.

- **Choose a Mindful Physical Activity:** Select a mindful physical activity that resonates with you. This could be yoga, Tai Chi, mindful walking, or any exercise that combines movement with mental presence.

- **Mindful Movement:** As you engage in your chosen activity, pay close attention to the sensations in your body. Notice how your body feels with each movement, and be fully present in the experience.

- **Focus on Your Breath:** Integrate conscious breathing into your physical activity. Sync your breath with your movements. Inhale deeply as you expand, and exhale slowly as you contract. This synchronized breath enhances mindfulness.

- **Mental Clarity:** As you practice mindful movement, aim to clear your mind of distractions. Let go of worries, to-do lists, and thoughts that may cloud your mental space. Focus on the present moment.

- **Embrace Relaxation:** Allow the physical activity to promote relaxation. Feel tension release from your muscles and notice a sense of calm washing over you.

- **Mind-Body Connection Reflection:** After your mindful physical activity, take a moment to reflect on the mind-body connection you experienced. Notice any shifts in your mental clarity, mood, or physical well-being.

- **Regular Practice:** Consider incorporating mindful movement into your daily routine or at least several times a week. Consistency in this practice will deepen your mind-body connection.

- **Integration into Your Routine:** Find a convenient time to integrate mindful physical activity into your daily routine. Whether it's a morning ritual or a midday break, choose a time that works best for you.

- **Patience and Self-Kindness:** Be patient with yourself and practice self-kindness. The mind-body connection may take time to strengthen, so embrace the journey without judgment.

Cultivating the mind-body connection through mindful physical activity is a valuable self-care practice. It not only enhances mental clarity but also promotes physical well-being. As you continue to integrate this practice into your routine, you'll discover the profound harmony between your mind and body, fostering a sense of balance in your life.

Day 4 – Emotional Wellness Check-In:

Now, I want to focus on nurturing your emotional wellness by conducting regular emotional check-ins. This practice helps you maintain awareness of your emotions and respond to them in a healthy and constructive manner.

- **Preparation for Emotional Check-In:** Begin by finding a quiet and comfortable space where you can conduct your emotional check-in without distractions. Have your journal or a notebook ready for this practice.

- **Reflect on Your Day:** Take a few moments to reflect on your day or any recent experiences. Consider the events, interactions, and situations that have occurred.

- **Identify Your Emotions:** Name and identify the emotions you've experienced throughout the day. Be specific and honest with yourself. Recognize both positive and challenging emotions.

- **Explore the Causes:** Examine the causes or triggers behind these emotions. Try to pinpoint what led to each emotion. This step enhances your self-awareness.

- **Emotional Journaling:** Write down your emotions and their causes in your journal. Use this space to express yourself honestly. This can be a powerful tool for emotional release and self-reflection.

- **Gratitude Practice:** Incorporate a gratitude practice into your emotional check-in. Reflect on the positive aspects of your day and the things you're grateful for. This helps maintain emotional balance.

- **Embrace Self-Compassion:** As you journal your emotions, practice self-compassion. Avoid self-criticism or judgment. Understand that it's okay to experience a range of emotions, and they provide valuable insights.

- **Self-Care Strategies:** Consider self-care strategies that can support your emotional well-being. This could involve practicing relaxation techniques, engaging in soothing activities, or seeking support from loved ones.

- **Commit to Regular Check-Ins:** Make a commitment to conduct regular emotional check-ins. You can do this at the end of each day or at specific times when you feel the need to connect with your emotions.

- **Adapt and Adjust:** Use your emotional check-ins as a tool for self-adjustment. If you notice patterns of emotions or triggers that require attention, consider adjusting your self-care routine or seeking professional support.

You nurture your emotional awareness and well-being by regularly checking in with your emotions and expressing them through journaling. This practice helps you maintain a balanced and harmonious relationship with your emotions, empowering you to respond to life's challenges with resilience and empathy.

Day 5 – Reflect and Adjust:

Today, I want your focus to be on reflection and adjustment to create a sustainable and holistic self-care routine. This practice empowers you to maintain a sense of balance and resilience in your daily life.

- **Set Aside Time for Reflection:** Allocate dedicated time for self-reflection. Find a quiet and comfortable space where you can think, write, and plan without distractions.
- **Review Your Week:** Begin by reviewing your self-care practices and experiences throughout the week. Consider the mindfulness, emotional awareness, physical activities, and self-love practices you've engaged in.
- **Reflect on Progress:** Take a moment to reflect on the progress you've made during this program. Celebrate your achievements and acknowledge any positive changes in your overall well-being.
- **Identify Challenges:** Recognize any challenges or obstacles you've encountered in maintaining your self-care routine. This self-awareness can help you address and overcome these challenges.

- **Adjust Your Routine:** Based on your reflections, consider adjustments to your self-care routine. Are there areas that require more attention or modifications? Be open to fine-tuning your practices.

- **Prioritize Self-Compassion:** Practice self-compassion throughout this process. Avoid self-criticism and perfectionism. Understand that self-care is a journey, and it's okay to adapt and grow along the way.

- **Create a Sustainable Plan:** Develop a sustainable self-care plan that integrates mindfulness, emotional wellness, physical well-being, and self-love practices. Ensure it aligns with your needs and goals.

- **Set Realistic Goals:** Set realistic and achievable self-care goals for the upcoming weeks. These goals should challenge you but also be attainable within your current lifestyle.

- **Implement Adjustments:** Start implementing the adjustments you've identified immediately. Whether it's allocating more time for self-care or trying new practices, take proactive steps.

- **Reflect Regularly:** Commit to regular reflections on your self-care journey. Make it a weekly or monthly practice to assess your progress and make necessary adjustments.

- **Embrace Consistency:** Consistency is critical to holistic self-care. Stay committed to your self-care routine, and over time, you'll reap the benefits of improved well-being.

By reflecting and adjusting your self-care routine, you create a sustainable and holistic approach to well-being. This practice empowers you to maintain balance in your life, navigate challenges with resilience, and continue your journey toward holistic self-care.

During this past week, we embarked on a journey of self-discovery and well-being as we explored the practices of integration and holistic self-care. These practices aim to nurture your physical, mental, and emotional well-being, fostering a sense of balance and resilience in your daily life.

This week served as a culmination of our self-care journey, highlighting the significance of holistic self-care in maintaining a balanced and resilient life. By integrating these practices into our daily lives, we've gained essential skills for navigating life's challenges with grace.

As we look ahead to Week 9, we'll focus on "Planning for the Future" and setting long-term self-care goals. This next step in our journey will empower us to envision and work towards a future filled with holistic well-being and self-care excellence. Stay tuned for another week of growth and self-discovery.

Week 9: Planning for the Future:

Welcome to Week 9, the final week of our "Mindful Living" journey. This week, we'll conclude our program by focusing on future planning, reflection, and setting long-term self-care goals.

Day 1 - Reflection:

Day 1 marks the beginning of our final week, and it's all about reflection. This practice is essential as it allows you to pause and reflect on your mindful living journey over the past eight weeks. Here's a detailed guide on how to make the most of this day:

- **Find a Quiet Space:** Start by finding a quiet and comfortable space where you can sit or lie down. This space should be free from distractions so that you can focus entirely on your reflection.

- **Close Your Eyes:** If you feel comfortable doing so, close your eyes. This can help you turn your attention inward and block out external distractions.

- **Take a Few Deep Breaths:** Begin by taking a few deep breaths to center yourself. Inhale deeply through your nose, counting to four as you do so. Then, exhale slowly through your mouth for a count of four. Repeat this a few times to calm your mind.

- **Review Your Journey:** With your eyes closed and your breathing steady, start to review your journey through the "Mindful Living" program. Recall the various practices, insights, and experiences you've had along the way. Consider how these practices have affected your well-being.

- **Embrace Gratitude:** As you reflect, embrace a sense of gratitude for the progress you've made. Acknowledge the efforts you've put into your self-care and mindfulness journey.

- **Note Challenges and Growth:** Be honest with yourself about any challenges you've encountered during the program. Reflect on how you've grown and what you've learned from facing these challenges.

- **Set Intentions:** As you conclude your reflection, set intentions for the final week and beyond. Think about what you hope to achieve in terms of self-care, mindfulness, and well-being.

- **Open Your Eyes:** When you feel ready, open your eyes and take a moment to ground yourself in the present moment.

- **Journal Your Reflections:** After your reflection, take some time to journal your thoughts and insights. Write down what stood out to you during your reflection, your intentions for the week, and any emotions that surfaced.

Remember, today is about looking back to move forward. By reflecting on your journey, you gain a deeper understanding of your progress and can set meaningful intentions for the final week and your ongoing self-care journey.

Day 2 - Document Progress:

Get your journal and a pen and we will dive into documenting your self-care progress. This practice is all about recognizing how far you've come and celebrating your growth. Here's a step-by-step guide to help you make the most of this day:

- **Create a Quiet Space**: Find a peaceful and comfortable place where you won't be disturbed. It's important to create an environment conducive to reflection.

- **Gather Your Materials:** Have your journal or a notebook, a pen, and any previous notes or reflections from the program ready.

- **Reflect on Your Journey:** Take a moment to sit quietly and recall the various practices, insights, and experiences you've had during the "Mindful Living" program. Consider how these practices have impacted your well-being and your understanding of mindfulness.

- **Review Your Journal:** If you've been keeping a journal throughout the program (which is highly recommended), go back and read your previous entries. Notice any patterns, shifts in your thinking, or moments of growth that you've documented.

- **Note Emotional Progress:** Pay special attention to your emotional progress. Have you become more aware of your emotions? Have you learned new ways to manage stress or cultivate self-compassion? Reflect on any emotional transformations you've undergone.

- **Celebrate Achievements:** Celebrate your achievements and milestones. Take time to acknowledge the efforts you've invested in your self-care journey and the positive changes you've witnessed.

- **Identify Areas for Improvement:** While celebrating your progress, also identify areas where you believe there is room for improvement. This is an opportunity for self-awareness and growth.

- **Set Future Goals:** Based on your reflection, set specific and realistic goals for your ongoing self-care journey. What would you like to achieve in terms of mindfulness, emotional well-being, and self-compassion in the future?

- **Journal Your Insights:** Use your journal to record your reflections, achievements, areas for improvement, and future goals. Writing down your thoughts can help solidify your intentions.

- **Embrace Gratitude:** End your session with gratitude. Express thankfulness for the progress you've made and the opportunity to continue your journey toward well-being.

- **Close Your Session:** When you're ready, close your session and take a few mindful breaths to ground yourself in the present moment.

Today has been is all about recognizing your growth and documenting it for future reference. It's a valuable practice for acknowledging your achievements, refining your goals, and preparing for the next phase of your self-care journey.

Day 3 - Long-Term Self-Care Goals:

It is now time to focus on setting long-term self-care goals to continue nurturing your well-being in the months and years ahead. This practice encourages you to envision your future and plan for sustained mindfulness and self-compassion. Here's a step-by-step guide to help you establish meaningful long-term goals:

- **Find a Tranquil Space:** Begin by finding a quiet and comfortable space where you can think and plan without distractions.

- **Reflect on Your Journey:** Take a moment to reflect on your "Mindful Living" journey so far. Consider the practices and insights that have resonated with you and how they have contributed to your well-being.

- **Visualize Your Future:** Close your eyes and visualize your future self. Imagine a version of you who embodies mindfulness, emotional awareness, and self-compassion. What does this future self look like? What qualities does it possess?

- **Set Specific Goals:** Based on your visualization, set specific long-term self-care goals. These goals should align with your vision of a more mindful and balanced life. Be precise about what you want to achieve.

- **Break Goals into Steps:** Break down each long-term goal into smaller, actionable steps. Think about what you need to do on a daily, weekly, or monthly basis to work toward these goals.

- **Prioritize Goals:** Consider which goals are most important to you and prioritize them. You may have several goals, but it's essential to focus your energy on the ones that matter most.

- **Set Realistic Timeframes:** Assign realistic timeframes to your goals. When do you hope to achieve them? Having deadlines can help you stay accountable.

- **Create an Action Plan:** Develop a practical action plan for each goal. What specific actions will you take to move closer to your objectives? Write these down.

- **Seek Accountability:** Consider whether you want to share your goals with a friend, family member, or mentor who can provide support and hold you accountable.

- **Record Your Goals:** Use your journal or a dedicated notebook to record your long-term self-care goals and action plans. Writing them down solidifies your commitment.

- **Embrace Positive Affirmations:** End your session with positive affirmations related to your goals. Affirmations can reinforce your belief in your ability to achieve them.

- **Close Your Session:** When you're ready, close your session by taking a few mindful breaths and grounding yourself in the present moment.

In summary, Day 3 helps you set long-term self-care goals and break them into actionable steps, providing a roadmap for a more mindful and balanced life.

Day 4 - Action Plan:

Our journey is all about turning your long-term self-care goals into actionable plans. An action plan is a structured approach to achieving your objectives. Here's how to create one:

- **Review Your Long-Term Goals:** Begin by revisiting the long-term self-care goals you set on Day 3. Refresh your memory about what you want to achieve in the future.

- **Break Goals into Smaller Steps:** Take each long-term goal and break it down into smaller, manageable steps. These steps should be specific and concrete, making it clear what you need to do.

- **Set Deadlines:** Assign deadlines to each of these smaller steps. Having deadlines creates a sense of urgency and helps you stay on track.

- **Prioritize Tasks:** Consider the order in which you'll tackle these steps. What should come first, second, and so on? Prioritizing tasks ensures a logical progression toward your goals.

- **Allocate Resources:** Identify any resources you'll need to accomplish each step. This might include time, money, knowledge, or support from others.

- **Identify Potential Challenges:** Anticipate potential challenges or obstacles that could arise along the way. Thinking ahead allows you to plan for how you'll overcome them.

- **Create a Timeline:** Develop a timeline or schedule that outlines when you'll work on each step. Be realistic about the time you can allocate to your goals.

- **Monitor Progress:** Regularly review your action plan and monitor your progress. Are you staying on schedule? Are there any adjustments needed?

- **Adjust as Necessary:** If you encounter unexpected challenges or changes in your circumstances, be flexible. Adjust your action plan as necessary to keep moving forward.

- **Seek Support:** Don't hesitate to seek support or guidance from friends, family, or professionals who can assist you in achieving your goals.

- **Stay Committed:** Commit to following your action plan diligently. Consistency is key to making progress.

- **Celebrate Milestones:** Celebrate your achievements along the way. Each completed step is a milestone toward your long-term goals.

By the end of Day 4, you should have a well-structured action plan that transforms your long-term self-care goals into a series of manageable tasks. This plan will guide you as you work towards a future filled with mindfulness and well-being. Tomorrow, Day 5, is where we'll wrap up our "Mindful Living" journey with a focus on celebrating your achievements and maintaining your self-care habits.

Day 5 - Celebrate and Maintain:

As we conclude our "Mindful Living" journey, Day 5 of Week 9 invites you to celebrate your achievements and commit to maintaining your self-care journey. It's a day of reflection, acknowledgment, and forward-looking commitment. Here's how to make the most of it:

- **Reflect on Your Journey:** Begin by reflecting on the entire nine-week journey. Consider the insights you've gained, the progress you've made, and the challenges you've overcome. Acknowledge your growth and the positive changes you've experienced.

- **Celebrate Your Achievements:** Take the time to celebrate your achievements. Recognize the milestones you've reached along the way. Whether it's improved mindfulness, better emotional awareness, or enhanced self-compassion, celebrate these victories.

- **Revisit Your Long-Term Goals:** Return to the long-term self-care goals you set on Day 3. Reaffirm your commitment to these goals and remind yourself why they are important to you.

- **Commit to Ongoing Self-Care:** Make a solemn commitment to continue your self-care journey. Recognize that self-care is an ongoing process, and the habits you've developed should be integrated into your daily life.

- **Establish a Maintenance Plan:** Develop a plan for maintaining the self-care practices you've cultivated. Consider how you will ensure these habits remain a consistent part of your routine.

- **Stay Connected:** Stay connected with your self-care community, whether it's friends, family, or fellow program participants. Share your experiences, offer support, and seek guidance when needed.

- **Embrace Growth:** Embrace the potential for ongoing growth and self-discovery. Understand that your self-care journey is not a destination but a lifelong commitment to your well-being.

- **Express Gratitude:** Express gratitude for the journey you've undertaken and the positive changes you've made in your life. Gratitude reinforces a positive outlook.

- **Look to the Future:** Look forward to the future with optimism and confidence. Your newfound self-care practices will serve as a strong foundation for facing life's challenges.

- **Continue to Celebrate:** As you move forward, continue to celebrate your achievements, no matter how small. Each day is an opportunity for growth and self-compassion.

As we bid farewell to this program, remember that self-care is not a one-time event but a lifelong commitment to your well-being. By celebrating your achievements and maintaining the habits you've developed, you'll continue to reap the rewards of a mindful and balanced life. Thank you for embarking on this transformative journey of self-discovery and mindfulness with us. Your dedication to self-care is a valuable investment in your overall happiness and resilience.

Conclusion: Empowering Yourself for the Future

Gandhi once said, *"The future depends on what you do today."* - (Gandhi)

Gandhi was a prominent leader in the Indian independence movement against British rule. He is renowned for his philosophy of nonviolent resistance, advocating for social and political change through peaceful means. His commitment to self-improvement, compassion, and personal empowerment made him a symbol of hope and inspiration worldwide.

Conclusion: Empowering Yourself for the Future

Maintaining and Growing Your Self-Care Practices

As we approach the conclusion of our journey together, it's vital to recognize that the end of this book is not the end of your self-care journey. The practices, insights, and habits you've developed are the foundation upon which you can continue to build a life filled with well-being and fulfillment. Maintaining and growing your self-care practices means integrating them into your everyday life. It's about making self-care not just an activity, but a way of being.

To sustain these practices, regularly revisit the strategies and lessons learned. Adapt them to evolving life circumstances and allow them to grow with you. Remember, self-care is a dynamic process, and your approach can change and evolve. Be open to trying new techniques, exploring different aspects of self-care, and continually seeking growth in this area.

Setting Vision and Goals for Future You

Looking forward, it's crucial to set a vision for what you want your life to look like. What are the values you want to live by? What are the qualities you wish to cultivate in yourself? These questions can guide you in setting meaningful and personal goals.

Create a vision board or journal about the 'future you.' Set goals that align with this vision, whether they involve personal development, career aspirations, relationships, or health.

Embracing Life's Journey with Confidence and Resilience

Embracing life's journey with confidence and resilience is about acknowledging that while life may bring challenges and uncertainties, you have the inner strength and tools to navigate them. It's about trusting in your ability to adapt and grow through whatever experiences come your way.

Confidence comes from recognizing your self-worth and abilities. Resilience is built through overcoming challenges and learning from them. Together, they empower you to face life with a positive and determined mindset. Remember, every challenge is an opportunity for growth, and every success is a testament to your resilience and strength.

Reflecting on Your Self-Care Journey

Take time to reflect on your self-care journey. Look back at where you started and acknowledge the progress you've made. Reflection allows you to appreciate your efforts, understand your growth, and learn from your experiences. Consider keeping a reflection journal where you can periodically write about your self-care journey. What practices have become integral to your life? What lessons have you learned about yourself? How has your approach to self-care changed your perspective on life?

Continuing Your Growth Beyond the Book

Your growth doesn't stop with the last page of this book. In fact, this is just the beginning. Continue to seek out resources, knowledge, and experiences that contribute to your personal growth. Engage in lifelong learning, whether through reading, courses, workshops, or conversations with others.

Seek communities and groups that align with your interests and values. Surround yourself with people who inspire and motivate you. Remember, growth is a continuous journey, not a destination.

A Final Word of Encouragement

As we part ways in this book, I leave you with a final word of encouragement: believe in yourself and the journey you are on. You have the power to create a life that resonates with joy, peace, and fulfillment. Your journey of self-care and personal growth is one of the most important journeys you will ever embark on. It's a path to discovering your true self, unlocking your potential, and living a life that is authentically yours.

Embrace each day with kindness towards yourself and others. Celebrate your victories, learn from your setbacks, and keep moving forward with hope and determination. You are capable of extraordinary things, and your journey is a beautiful testament to the strength and resilience that lies within you.

Thank you for allowing me to be a part of your journey. May you continue to thrive, grow, and shine in all you do. Remember, the best is yet to come.

We'd Love to Hear Your Story!

Hey there, Amazing Reader!

You've just turned the last page of "Nine Self-Care Essentials," we invite you to take a moment to reflect on the entirety of your journey with us. You've now traversed the entire landscape of our book, rich with insights and transformative wisdom. Your experiences and reflections are more than just valuable feedback for us; they are guiding lights for fellow travelers on their own quests for growth and self-discovery.

How has this complete journey resonated with you? Did the chapters collectively inspire a shift in your life, bring about newfound understanding, or offer solace during times of reflection? The story of your journey shared through your feedback, becomes a powerful beacon of hope and guidance for others. It's a testament to the shared human experience, connecting readers in a web of shared narratives and mutual growth.

We encourage you to take a brief moment to leave a review. This is your opportunity to express your complete thoughts, insights, and any transformative experiences you've had. Your words hold the power to uplift, resonate, and foster a community that values shared wisdom and supportive connections.

Thank you for walking this path with us. Your voice is vital to this journey, not just for us but for the many readers who will follow in your footsteps.

Love it? Leave a Review

With Deepest Appreciation,

Eliza Bennet & Inspire Self Growth Publishing

Bibliography

Brownn, E. (n.d.). p.135.

Buddha. (n.d.). p.61.

Chopra, D. (n.d.). p.85.

Churchill, W. (n.d.). p.95.

Dyer, D. W. (n.d.). p.125.

Franklin, B. (n.d.). p.47.

Gandhi, M. (n.d.). p.261.

Hạnh, T. N. (2013). *Peace Is Every Step.* Bantam/AJP p.5.

James, W. (n.d.). p.91.

Maraboli, S. (2014). *Life, The Truth , & Being Free.* A Better Today p.1.

Reed, K. (n.d.). p123.

Rogers, C. R. (1961). *On Becoming a Person: A Therapist's View of Phychotherapy.* London: Constable & Co p.21.

Recommended Reading

Bradshaw, J. (2005). Healing the Shame that Binds You. Deerfield Beach, FL: Health Communications.

Bridges, W. (2004). Transitions: Making Sense of Life's Changes. Cambridge, MA: Da Capo Press.

Brown, B. (2010). The Gifts of Imperfection: Let Go of Who You Think You're Supposed to Be and Embrace Who You Are. Center City, MN: Hazelden Publishing.

Brown, B. (2012). Daring Greatly: How the Courage to Be Vulnerable Transforms the Way We Live, Love, Parent, and Lead. New York, NY: Gotham Books.

Burns, D. D. (1999). The Feeling Good Handbook. New York, NY: Plume.

Chödrön, P. (2000). When Things Fall Apart: Heart Advice for Difficult Times. Boston, MA: Shambhala Publications.

Chopra, D. (1990). Quantum Healing: Exploring the Frontiers of Mind/Body Medicine. New York, NY: Bantam Books.

Covey, S. R. (1989). The 7 Habits of Highly Effective People: Powerful Lessons in Personal Change. New York, NY: Simon & Schuster.

Davis, M., Eshelman, E. R., & McKay, M. (2008). The Relaxation and Stress Reduction Workbook. Oakland, CA: New Harbinger Publications.

Deschene, L. (2010). Tiny Buddha: Simple Wisdom for Life's Hard Questions. San Francisco, CA: HarperOne.

Dossey, L. (1993). Healing Words: The Power of Prayer and the Practice of Medicine. San Francisco, CA: HarperSanFrancisco.

Dweck, C. S. (2006). Mindset: The New Psychology of Success. New York, NY: Random House.

Ford, D. (2001). The Dark Side of the Light Chasers: Reclaiming Your Power, Creativity, Brilliance, and Dreams. New York, NY: Riverhead Books.

Germer, C. K. (2009). The Mindful Path to Self-Compassion: Freeing Yourself from Destructive Thoughts and Emotions. New York, NY: Guilford Press.

Gilbert, E. (2006). Eat, Pray, Love: One Woman's Search for Everything Across Italy, India and Indonesia. New York, NY: Penguin Books.

Goldstein, J. (2013). Mindfulness: A Practical Guide to Awakening. Boulder, CO: Sounds True.

Hanson, R. (2013). Hardwiring Happiness: The New Brain Science of Contentment, Calm, and Confidence. New York, NY: Harmony.

Hanh, T. N. (1999). The Miracle of Mindfulness: An Introduction to the Practice of Meditation. Boston, MA: Beacon Press.

Harris, R. (2008). The Happiness Trap: How to Stop Struggling and Start Living: A Guide to ACT. Boston, MA: Trumpeter.

Hayes, S. C., & Smith, S. (2005). Get Out of Your Mind and Into Your Life: The New Acceptance and Commitment Therapy. Oakland, CA: New Harbinger Publications.

Kabat-Zinn, J. (1990). Full Catastrophe Living: Using the Wisdom of Your Body and Mind to Face Stress, Pain, and Illness. New York, NY: Delta.

Kabat-Zinn, J. (1994). Wherever You Go, There You Are: Mindfulness Meditation in Everyday Life. New York, NY: Hyperion.

Kempton, S. (2013). Meditation for the Love of It: Enjoying Your Own Deepest Experience. Boulder, CO: Sounds True.

Kessler, D. (2020). Finding Meaning: The Sixth Stage of Grief. New York, NY: Scribner.

Lipton, B. H. (2005). The Biology of Belief: Unleashing the Power of Consciousness, Matter & Miracles. Santa Rosa, CA: Mountain of Love/Elite Books.

McGonigal, K. (2015). The Upside of Stress: Why Stress Is Good for You, and How to Get Good at It. New York, NY: Avery.

Myss, C. (1996). Anatomy of the Spirit: The Seven Stages of Power and Healing. New York, NY: Harmony Books.

Neff, K. (2011). Self-Compassion: The Proven Power of Being Kind to Yourself. New York, NY: William Morrow.

Posen, D. B. (2013). Is Work Killing You?: A Doctor's Prescription for Treating Workplace Stress. Toronto, Canada: House of Anansi Press.

Pert, C. B. (1997). Molecules of Emotion: The Science Behind Mind-Body Medicine. New York, NY: Scribner.

Ruiz, D. M. (1997). The Mastery of Love: A Practical Guide to the Art of Relationship. San Rafael, CA: Amber-Allen Publishing.

Salzberg, S. (2011). Real Happiness: The Power of Meditation: A 28-Day Program. New York, NY: Workman Publishing Company.

Seligman, M. E. P. (2002). Authentic Happiness: Using the New Positive Psychology to Realize Your Potential for Lasting Fulfillment. New York, NY: Free Press.

Siegel, D. J. (2010). Mindsight: The New Science of Personal Transformation. New York, NY: Bantam Books.

van der Kolk, B. (2014). The Body Keeps the Score: Brain, Mind, and Body in the Healing of Trauma. New York, NY: Viking.

Young, E. (2012). The Self-Love Experiment: Fifteen Principles for Becoming More Kind, Compassionate, and Accepting of Yourself. New York, NY: TarcherPerigee.